AN HONOURABLE ESTATE

AN HONOURABLE ESTATE

The doctrine of Marriage according to English law and the obligation of the Church to marry all parishioners who are not divorced

The Report of a Working Party established by the Standing Committee of the General Synod of the Church of England

GS 801
This Report has only the authority of the Working Party which prepared it

CHURCH HOUSE PUBLISHING
Church House, Great Smith Street, London SW1P 3NZ

ISBN 0 7151 3719 0

Published 1988 for the General Synod of the Church of England
by Church House Publishing

Printed in England by The Ludo Press Ltd, London SW18 3DG

Contents

Preface

The members of the Working Party set out on their task holding different opinions on what policy the Church should follow today in the context of changing contemporary attitudes and laws concerning marriage. In the light of the evidence which we received and through careful and lengthy debate the Working Party came to a common mind. We wish to emphasise, however, that it was our purpose, directed by our terms of reference, to lay before the Church the factual evidence on marriage from theology, history, the law and social practice. We hope and pray that our work will facilitate informed discussion so that the Church of England can formulate a marriage policy which will hold loyally to the gospel of Jesus Christ and pursue his mission to our nation.

It is appropriate to express the Church's gratitude to the members of the Working Party who have given time from very full lives to the work which the General Synod requested.

We wish to record thanks to Prebendary John Gladwin, kindly made available by the Board for Social Responsibility, and to Mr David Hebblethwaite, our Secretary; to both much of the background research and drafting of this Report was committed. We also wish to note our thanks to Miss Michèle McLaughlin for patiently and efficiently handling the large quantity of paper generated by our work.

TIMOTHY HOARE

Members of the Working Party

Sir Timothy Hoare Bt (Chairman)
Professor Peter Bromley, Emeritus Professor of English Law,
    Manchester University
Mr John Bullimore, Barrister, Chancellor of the Diocese of Derby
The Rt Revd Peter Coleman, Bishop of Crediton
The Rt Revd Michael Mann, Dean of Windsor
Mrs Rachel Nugee JP, Past Central President of the Mothers' Union
Lady Oppenheimer, Writer on Christian Ethics

CONSULTANT

Sir William van Straubenzee MBE, formerly MP for Wokingham
    and Second Church Estates Commissioner

STAFF IN ATTENDANCE

Mr Derek Pattinson, Secretary-General of the General Synod
Prebendary John Gladwin, Secretary, Board for Social Responsibility
Mr Brian Hanson, Registrar and Legal Adviser to the General Synod
Mr David Hebblethwaite, General Synod Office (Secretary to
    the Working Party)

Introduction

1.   In February 1984 the Bishop of Chichester successfully moved a motion in the General Synod in the following terms:

that the Synod

. . . (iii) asks the Standing Committee to review and report on the effect of recent and current changes in society and in the Marriage law and the growing number of divorces on the doctrine of Marriage according to English law and the obligation of the Church to marry all parishioners who are not divorced.

As the result of this motion the Standing Committee established the Working Party whose membership is shown on page viii. That Working Party now presents its Report.

2.   The Bishop of Chichester's motion was passed in the context of a debate about the marriage in church of those who had been divorced and whose previous partner was still living. This matter had been under more or less constant discussion since the report of the Marriage Commission, chaired by the Rt Revd K. J. F. Skelton, then Bishop of Lichfield, which had appeared in 1978. That Commission began its report with the words 'This report is about marriage' and considered the implications of the growing number of divorces for Christian understanding of the institution. It concluded that there were circumstances in which the second marriages of those who had been divorced could be solemnised in a church. Subsequent attempts to establish criteria for regulating which of these marriages should be so solemnised have foundered. In the meantime the number of divorces has continued to rise and there have been further legislative changes (see Chapter 3).

3.   A further thread in the debate since 1978 emerged in a private member's motion in General Synod in the name of Canon Douglas Rhymes that:

. . . this Synod, in view of the present position regarding Marriage disciplines in the Church:

(a) would favour the consideration of a system of universal civil marriage in England.

(b) requests the Standing Committee to investigate and report to the Synod the implications of such a system for the Marriage disciplines of the Church.

This had gathered sufficient support to be due for debate in February 1985 (when this working party was but newly established). Rather than add further to the debates on this matter it was accepted that we would include the terms of Canon Rhymes's motion within our remit.

4.   We were set up as a working party in January 1985 and have met seventeen times; six meetings have been residential.

THE SCOPE OF THE EVIDENCE

5.   In February 1985 an invitation for the submission of written evidence was given wide circulation in newspapers and journals. A good many submissions were received in response to this invitation and they are listed in Appendix 4. We take this opportunity of thanking all those who contributed such written evidence. It has all been carefully considered and most of it has been helpful to our working.

6.   In the course of our work we met and consulted representatives of a number of bodies and some individuals; these are listed in Appendix 5. The reasons which prompted us to seek out these particular expressions of view are touched on in the following paragraphs. We are particularly grateful to those who, at our request, gave generously of their time to meet us.

7.   Our visitors included both the Bishop of Chichester, who has been to the fore in matters of Canon law for many years, and Canon Rhymes, now retired, but with many years' practical experience as a parish priest both in inner London and rural Surrey. They were able to speak to us of the reasons which lay behind the tabling of the motions which form our terms of reference.

8.   The Mothers' Union, on hearing of the setting up of the working party, put in hand a survey, widely distributed amongst its members, on the matters covered by our work. When Mrs Hazel Treadgold, the Central President of the Mothers' Union, came to meet us, she was able to bring with her a summary of the results of that survey and this is included in Appendix 2. We recognised in this survey a significant expression of view from a large sample of active lay people in the Church of England. We also sought out, and were glad to hear, an expression of view from outside the Church's tradition. Dr Tessa Blackstone (now

Baroness Blackstone of Stoke Newington and Master of Birkbeck College) spoke forcefully for those for whom the Church's traditional views on marriage have little power to convince.

9. We invited four parochial clergy, named in Appendix 5, as representative of the attitudes expressed in the written evidence we had received, to propound their views in discussion with us and with each other. We recognise the importance of hearing and appreciating the views of the clergy who are currently operating the marriage discipline of the Church. Our four visitors brought to the discussion different attitudes and conclusions from their experience of working in parishes in London, Bristol, Manchester and Sheffield.

10. We came to feel, at an early stage, that we needed to have more knowledge of the operation of Church marriage discipline in situations where there is no obligation for clergy to solemnise the marriages of all parishioners who ask. We also wanted to know what happens in those countries where there is the requirement of a civil marriage ceremony in addition to any religious ceremony. Thus we sought to learn from the Free Churches and the Roman Catholic Church in England. The Revd Gerald Burt, of the Methodist Division of Social Affairs, had taken soundings from other Free Churches before meeting us and Monsignor Ronald Brown and Judge Baker spoke not only from a knowledge of the Roman Catholic Canon law but also from experience with the large and diverse Roman Catholic community in England. (Judge Baker is a Marriage Guidance counsellor of long standing.) We also sought information from other countries in Europe whose traditions and practice differ from ours. We asked for, and were kindly supplied with, written statements of their discipline and policy by the Church authorities in a number of European countries. These written statements were most valuably illuminated and filled out for us by the visit of Fr Jan Kerkhofs SJ, Professor at the University of Leuven (Louvain), (who formerly edited the valuable Europe-wide survey of opinion 'Pro Mundi Vita') and Professor Doctor Dieter Giesen, Professor für Privatrechtsvergleichung in the Free University of West Berlin (a Roman Catholic layman). We are especially grateful to these visitors from overseas.

11. We were grateful for the opportunity of meeting representatives of the Society of Registration Officers. This gave us some understanding of the practical operation of civil marriage in England. We were pleased to find that they, for their own part, were glad of the opportunity to

exchange views with us and to impress on the Church the importance of accurate and consistent standards of registration, whilst recognising that for the clergy this will always be but one aspect of their function in solemnising marriages.

12.   We were indebted to Mr David Price, the Registrar of Wandsworth County Court, and a pioneer in improved conciliation services, for meeting us and for inviting the Chairman and Secretary to join him in his court. We also profited, in this part of our work, from hearing the views of Mr Nicholas Tyndall, then National Officer of the National Marriage Guidance Council, and from our close liaison with the House of Bishops' Marriage Education Panel and its adviser, the Revd Peter Chambers.

13.   On the evidence for current social trends, we were well served by Mrs Muriel Nissel, of the Policy Studies Institute; Mr Malcolm Wicks, of the Family Policy Studies Centre; and Mr John Haskey, statistician in the Registrar General's Department (whose lucid and meticulous interpretation of official statistics in the area with which we have been most concerned has been of great service).

14.   On the place of marriage in English law we were starkly but valuably made aware by Mrs, now Professor, Brenda Hoggett, as a member of the Law Commission, of the essentially reactive role taken by that Commission in matters of social policy. She emphasised that in the Commission's view there are limits to the part which law can play in moulding social attitudes (even though there are widespread expectations that law should reflect a 'view' of marriage). Ultimately, it is held, it must be the prevailing views amongst the population at large which influence changes in the law. The law provides the mechanism for contracting and dissolving marriages and makes provision for those within the married state. It does not, of itself, state a 'view' of marriage. The law is, moreover, of general application and may sometimes work unfairly, detrimentally or undesirably in particular cases.

15.   In the light of this understanding of the proper place of the law (an understanding with which not all of us were in sympathy) we must draw attention to the absence from our terms of reference of any mention of 'the state', though it is a term frequently used in the evidence we have received and which we have found it difficult to avoid in discussion and even in this Report. Any suggestion of a juxtaposition of 'Church' and 'state' views on marriage is misleading. The Church is one

element within a diverse and multifarious society and does not itself always project a single and simple view of marriage; there is a wide range of popular, though imprecise, expressions of opinion ascribed to those who are seen as outside and over against the Church, but no one voice which can provide an opposing 'state' view of marriage. There are aspects of government administration which bear on marriage, but no one organ or body which officially formulates or interprets what marriage is.

16.   We were helped in our discussions by meeting the Rt Revd Hugh Montefiore (then Bishop of Birmingham), and Sir William van Straubenzee (then Second Church Estates Commissioner). They reminded us that the Church's duties and obligations apply more widely than to marriage alone. The parishioner's claim extends to baptism and burial as well as marriage in church and all three spring out of, and reflect, the obligation laid on the Church to minister the good news of Christ to all citizens of this land who are willing to hear it. Although we have been aware that there are links with wider issues of the established position of the Church within society, we have properly limited our consideration to the question of marriage, as envisaged by our terms of reference.

THE SCOPE OF THE REPORT

17.   In the chapters which follow we seek first and foremost to place our work in a theological context (Chapter 1). We have not sought to do again the work achieved by earlier Reports but we have been mindful, throughout, of the primary place which rightly belongs to theology in any assessment of the doctrine of marriage. In the following chapters we first place the investigation into its historical and international context (Chapter 2), describe the legal position (Chapter 3), and outline the statistical information (Chapter 4) from which we have tried to establish the 'effect of recent and current changes in society'. In our final chapter we review the possible ways in which the Church might seek to react to the current position and make our unanimous recommendation.

CHAPTER 1

Theological Considerations

OUR CONTEXT

18.   This Report is about marriage, both as a divine and as a human institution. The Christian Church brings its distinctive interpretation to the institution, grounded in biblical insights: when husband and wife are joined in matrimony they become one flesh. There are other views on marriage, widely held in twentieth-century England, which are not so informed by traditional insights; and for many holding such views the bond created would not be thought so firm as to be described as 'one flesh'. Entry into the married state in English law is by various routes, both ecclesiastical and civil, but no distinction is made in law between different ways of understanding marriage. It is because there are some who would strongly urge that such a distinction should be made in present-day circumstances that we were established as a group in the way outlined in the Introduction to this Report.

19.   The concern and anxiety, which are indicated in both the motions which form our terms of reference, reflect the extent of the tensions and discomfort to which the Church's involvement in marriage in present-day circumstances gives rise. So does the failure to reach any consensus on the method by which divorced people might be allowed to marry in church. Indeed it was these same anxieties which led the General Synod to set up the Lichfield Commission which reported in 1978,[1] and which before that led the Archbishop of Canterbury to set up the Root Commission which reported in 1971.[2] We recognise that this Report will not, of itself, remove those tensions or ease all the discomfort. We do, however, trust that we will set the difficulties in a more clearly described context than sometimes appears to be the case.

---

[1] *Marriage and the Church's Task*, CIO Publishing 1978
[2] *Marriage, Divorce and the Church*, SPCK 1971

20. It is not our intention to attempt a new and substantial piece of theology on the subject of marriage. A great deal of work has been done on this in recent times including the two reports referred to above. It is beyond our scope to retread that ground. It is, however, our task to recall those features of the tradition and recent contributions which do bear on our terms of reference and to indicate our judgment on them.

OUR TRADITION

21. The understanding of marriage which has been held by the Church of England is contained in the Form of Solemnisation of Matrimony in the Book of Common Prayer. In the introduction to that service we are told that matrimony was 'instituted by God in the time of man's innocency, signifying unto us the mystical union that is betwixt Christ and his Church'. Two points come out here: that marriage is distinctively human, not specifically Christian; and that this universal human institution is capable of bearing Christian meaning. Canon B 30.1 sets out the nature and the purposes of marriage as God ordained it:

> The Church of England affirms, according to our Lord's teaching, that marriage is in its nature a union permanent and life-long, for better for worse, till death them do part, of one man with one woman, to the exclusion of all others on either side, for the procreation and nurture of children, for the hallowing and right direction of the natural instincts and affections, and for the mutual society, help and comfort which the one ought to have of the other, both in prosperity and adversity.[1]

22. The Canon reiterates the ends or purposes of marriage, as set out in the introduction to the 1928 Prayer Book (and later Series 1) service for marriage. The Alternative Service Book reaffirms these themes. Marriage, it affirms, is, 'a gift of God in creation and a means of his grace'. In it the partners are joined together to become 'one flesh'. The ASB has changed the Prayer Book order of the purposes of marriage, setting them out as: the comfort and help the couple have from each other, their coming together in bodily union, and the blessing of having children to be brought up to the praise and glory of God.

23. The theology of marriage in our tradition, therefore, is rooted in creation. The Old Testament teaching is picked up and illuminated in the New Testament (e.g. Mark 10.2–12). The nature of marriage is

---

[1] All the Canons which touch on marriage are reproduced in Appendix 3.

the 'one flesh' relationship. The outcome of marriage is the shared support and love of the couple, their bodily union and the establishment of their family.

THE CONCERN OF CHURCH AND SOCIETY

24. We need to think about marriage both as institution and as relationship. We may say that the 'form' of marriage is the institution and the 'content' of marriage is the relationship. How has the Church seen the connection between these? The Report of the Root Commission on the Christian doctrine of marriage, *Marriage, Divorce and the Church*, discussed this question illuminatingly, and we refer readers to it. Marriage as a relationship, it says, 'imperceptibly but inevitably' becomes an institution (para. 86).

> For all its richness, the personal factor cannot be the only consideration. Society, as well as the parties, has an interest in marriage. In simple terms, the day-to-day conduct of life in society, its ethics, rests on common expectations, and there must be some minimal certainties. It is necessary, for social purposes, to know who is to be accounted married to whom at any given time; without this knowledge intolerable personal and social conflicts could arise. (para. 90)

> Marriage and the family belong to the natural order. The State may rightly, therefore, be expected to have jurisdiction over them. It may rightly be expected to support and strengthen them where necessary, partly through the enactment of laws of various sorts, partly through the enabling and fostering of those conventions, voluntary associations, social rituals, and the like, which, in a healthy society, make intrusive law to a large extent unnecessary. (para. 100)

25. We should wish to endorse this. Then we would add that consideration of the institution should lead us back to the essential relationship between the couple. Thus when the Root Commission described the marks of the relationship in marriage as 'exclusiveness', 'commitment' and 'permanency', it was setting out some of the tests by which the adequacy of the institutional arrangements for marriage must be judged by Christians. Does marriage as provided for in our society encourage and support these essential qualities in the marriage relationship? It is not surprising, when faced with the evidence of social trends and with developments both in the content and procedure of the law in recent years, that the Church grows increasingly anxious about the health of marriage in our society today.

TWO APPROACHES

26.   At this point the Church has to make a central choice. Are we to go on being concerned for the state of marriage generally in our society? Why should we bother to press these Christian perceptions upon the whole community? Ought we to admit that what Christians mean by marriage is, after all, something different from what many of our contemporaries mean? The choice is between either taking up a doctrine of Christian marriage, and leaving the others to go their own way, or pursuing a Christian understanding of marriage, which is applicable to everyone. The doctrine and practice of the Church of England has long held to the second of these two approaches. The high and demanding doctrine of marriage set out in the formularies of the Church is a description of marriage as God has ordained it for the benefit of all. Whenever two people enter into 'a union permanent and life-long, for better for worse, till death them do part . . . both in prosperity and adversity', they are entering marriage as understood by the Church.

27.   The alternative approach of seeking for and holding to a doctrine of Christian marriage lies at the heart of some of the demands made for a radical break between the Church and the rest of society. If people hold either that marriage as understood in the Christian tradition is only available to Christians, or that Christians may only enter Christian marriage through the ministry of the Church, then there is bound to be pressure to make a clear distinction between civil and religious marriage. Thus it is being argued that there should be universal civil marriage to meet the needs of people throughout our society and that if couples want Christian marriage they will have to come to the Church for the appropriate Christian rites and ceremonies.

28.   We are bound to point out that this would be a major and radical shift of theological approach by the Church of England. We further believe that it would involve a departure from the teaching contained in the Book of Common Prayer. There is no suggestion in this tradition that the Christian doctrine of marriage means either that marriage is exclusive to Christians or that it is an exclusively Christian institution.

THE MEANING OF MARRIAGE

29.   What are the theological roots from which the tradition of the Church of England has grown? Let us take in turn the two phrases of the Prayer Book introduction, 'instituted of God in the time of man's innocency' and 'signifying unto us the mystical union that is betwixt Christ and his Church'.

'Instituted of God'

30.   The teaching of Jesus as recorded in the Gospels on the subject of marriage did not set up a new institution, but takes us back to the stories of creation in Genesis 1 and 2. The Christian description of marriage as a voluntary union for life between one man and one woman, to the exclusion of all others, has its roots in these early biblical stories. 'For this reason a man will leave his father and mother and be united to his wife, and they will become one flesh' (Gen. 2.24).[1]

Hugh Montefiore, commenting on this passage,[2] says

Most probably, the phrase 'one flesh', although it contained undoubtedly a sexual connotation, referred to the new family unit which is created when a woman leaves her family home to join her bridegroom. She becomes as it were 'flesh of his flesh' and he in turn 'cleaves' to her. The Hebrew word here is not sexual in meaning; it signifies to 'cling on to, to stick to' someone, when it is used of persons. It is this word which proves from Scripture the permanence of marriage.

The form of marriage is the leaving of parents and the joining together of the couple. The substance is the 'one flesh' relationship to which they are called. The institution of marriage is given by God in the creation of human life. Whoever, therefore, enters into this estate is entering a divine order. It is a gift of God for the benefit of all.

31.   According to this understanding, the Christian tradition affirms that when Christians enter marriage they are entering into an institution which God has created and which is common to human life. People of Christian faith, no faith, or of other faiths enter into the created order of marriage whenever they commit themselves to this relationship. What essentially makes a true marriage is not the Church's rites and ceremonies, nor even the couple's faith in God, but their consent to a lifelong union.

'Mystical Union'

32.   The second aspect of the tradition as it is affirmed in the Church of

---

[1] Von Rad, in commenting on this text, says: 'The story is entirely aetiological, i.e. it was told to answer a quite definite question. A fact needs explanation, namely, the extremely powerful drive of the sexes to each other. Whence comes this love "strong as death" (Song of Solomon 9) . . . It comes from the fact that God took woman from man and they actually were originally one flesh. Therefore they must come together again and thus by destiny they belong to each other . . . The alliance of one sex to another is seen as a divine ordinance of creation.' (*Genesis*, Gerhard von Rad, SCM, p.85)
[2] *Marriage, Divorce and the Church*, Appendix 1, p.81

England picks up the teaching of St Paul on marriage as set out in Ephesians 5: Here we are given a powerful testimony to the way in which human marriage can illumine divine reality. Marriage is able to be a sign of the love which Christ has for the Church and of the indestructible bond between Christ and the Church. Christians understand marriage to be patterned on the love of God. The love which binds husband and wife together must aspire to that quality of love with which Christ gave himself for others and which bonds the Church to God himself. That exclusive, committed and permanent relationship of marriage is to be lived out in response to the love of God as seen in Jesus Christ.

33. It is because marriage has been understood in the Christian tradition as a sign of the love between Christ and his Church that the Church has long used sacramental language and imagery to describe the nature of the marriage bond. Those who, in the light of the Gospel, covenant together as man and wife, are to be assured, in the words of the marital blessing of the Book of Common Prayer, that God will fill them 'with all spiritual benediction and grace'.

34. In the current authorised English translation of Roman Catholic Canon Law (1983),[1] Canon 1055 speaks of the Matrimonial Covenant as raised by Christ to the dignity of a sacrament. There is, of course, a long history of discussion between the Catholic and Protestant Churches about the nature and number of the sacraments and differing views on this matter are to be found among Anglicans. That discussion cannot be adequately reviewed here; it is sufficient, for our purpose, to note that those who seek God's blessing on their marriage will receive his grace.

35. Marital grace is often understood to be available only to Christians through the sacramental sign of the priestly blessing of the marriage, but sacramental language is being used here in the Roman tradition in a special sense. Marriage is the only sacrament where the parties themselves are the ministers, the priest acting as prime witness to it. Although the teaching of the Western Church on the sacramental nature of marriage can be found as early as the ninth century, by Hincmar of Rheims for example, and received powerful exposition by St Thomas

---

[1] Canons 1055–1060 of 1983 set out more fully the present rules of the Roman Catholic Church and reflect much of the history discussed in Chapter 2 of this Report.

Aquinas, this did not of itself provide the main reason for marriages being held in church, as is explained more fully in Chapter 2.

36.   It is significant that the Roman Canon 1055, referred to above (para. 34), preserves this traditional understanding. It states that the matrimonial covenant is established by the man and the woman, and Canon 1108 requires a priest or deacon and two other witnesses to be present to assist, while Canon 1112 allows a diocesan bishop discretion to delegate a lay person to assist at marriages where priests or deacons are lacking.

37.   A modern Roman Catholic discussion[1] of the nature of marital grace emphasises the principle that grace does not destroy nature but fulfils and transforms it. It is not imposed by the Church or the priest from outside the marriage, but comes from within, released so to speak by the couple's intention to create a marriage in Christ.

38.   The Church of England is not tied to this particular tradition but, as the matrimonial blessing in the Book of Common Prayer mentioned above (para. 35) and its modern equivalent in the Alternative Service Book both show, its liturgies affirm that there is something profoundly sacramental about marriage. It can truly be a 'means of grace'. Husbands and wives can be ministers of grace to one another, and when they are Christians they can be aware that marriage for them is a real channel of the grace of God.

39.   While holy matrimony is distinguished from the dominical sacraments of Baptism and Holy Communion in the teaching of the Church of England, there are important aspects of the marriage service which point towards its sacramental character. The joining of hands and the giving of rings are powerful outward and visible signs of the inward reality of the marriage made by the vows the couple have just exchanged. The Church, through its rites, expresses a characteristically Christian interpretation of marriage and thereby enables Christians who enter into it to find grace and encouragement for their union in Christ.

40.   We are far from wanting to minimise the idea of the Church as a radical community which lives the life of grace, whose standards are not

---

[1] See *Sacramentum Mundi*, ed. K. Rahner (Burns and Oates 1968) vol. 3 and *Marriage: Human Reality and Saving Mystery*, E. Schillebeeckx, Sheed & Ward 1965.

those of the secular world. What we want to deny is that this Christian community must have its own kind of marriage, any more than it must have, for instance, its own political party or its own shops. If Christians can hope to transform the institutions of the secular world, it is by filling whatever they do with the Christian spirit, not by claiming a monopoly of God's grace for their own activities. They are, as it were, more like leaven than a task force.

41. We would go further and assert that marriage is particularly unsuitable for the claiming of a Christian monopoly, when the union of husband and wife, as it has been known to human beings since before the dawn of history, is (at its best) a living parable in which human grace gives people a glimpse of what divine grace is like. This is not a low view of marriage, but a high one. The more one wants to emphasise the sacramental character of marriage, the more it needs to have strong human meaning. It is because husbands and wives love each other 'for better, for worse' that marriage can be an image of the love of Christ for the Church.

42. The two complementary aspects of the teaching of the Church of England, the stress on creation and on the sacramental character of marriage, set the boundaries of our doctrine. Within these boundaries it is to be expected that different groups and traditions will offer a variety of interpretations of this teaching. A further question remains: how is such a tradition to be deployed by the Church in the changing social context of its mission? The position we take in response to our terms of reference is set out in the final chapter. The basis for that is an acceptance on our part that the Church is always having to interpret its given tradition in the social context. The chapter on history gives an indication of how the Church, with various degrees of success, has sought to relate its Christian understanding to the changing experience of marriage as witnessed to in customs, laws, and social trends. If the sacramental side of our doctrine reminds us to guard the distinctive character of our understanding of marriage, the rooting of our doctrine in creation reminds us of the continual need to be sensitive and creative in interpreting the experience of marriage for all who enter into it. We cannot escape the dialectic between the tradition and our history. In carrying forward this interpretative task in the light of the demands placed upon us we see no reason for a radical shift in the tradition of the Church of England in its theological understanding of marriage. Indeed, we would want to reaffirm it and see it deployed for the well-being of all married people and their families in our time.

CHAPTER 2

Historical and International Perspectives

I HISTORICAL BACKGROUND

43.   Although the Group's terms of reference (as set out in the Introduction, paras. 1 and 3), are firmly rooted in the present or very recent past ('recent and current changes', 'growing number of divorces') there can be no balanced assessment of these contemporary factors without some appreciation of the historical background which has led up to them, and the need to take account of history bears on our analysis and recommendations. Any proposed changes, made in response to these current circumstances, are likely to gain acceptance only in so far as they take seriously the historical processes that appear to be at work.

44.   These historical developments, moulding and influencing our current attitudes and practice, are complex, and this Report is not the appropriate place for a full and detailed treatment of them. A number of scholarly studies are available and we draw attention to some of these in the bibliography in Appendix 6. In many ways present-day understanding of self and society differs significantly from that of times past. If we seek to impose contemporary values on the evidence from history, our understanding of past times is distorted and our understanding of the circumstances of the present day is limited.

The Christian Tradition

45.   Christianity was born into a world with a long history of marriage laws and customs. Judaism, Hellenistic culture and the widely prevalent Roman legal system intermingled in the cities where the Apostles preached. The high Patrician doctrines of earlier times, designed to preserve family status and property and stressing monogamy, permanence and fidelity had been largely eroded among the Romans. Greece contributed either ascetic scorn of the flesh or a liberalism which became positive with regard to the role of women in the community, but lax in its adherence to older traditions of sexual morality. Judaism, in principle, set down strong respect for home and family ties – these were

signs of God's commitment to Israel – and the practice of polygamy had waned. All three cultures maintained some of the ancient attitudes towards the inferior status of women and the double standard concerning adultery.

46.   Some features of the procedures for establishing a marriage were, broadly speaking, common to all three cultures. The initial commitment or betrothal was normally accompanied by some measure of family agreement, marriage contract and dowry. Betrothal could not be lightly set aside, and led to the marriage proper which was almost always effected by the physical move of the new bride into the husband's home, an occasion for procession and feasting. Religious ceremonial, including prayers of blessing on the new couple, were often included, but the rough and ready rule was that voluntary cohabitation, publicly entered into, created the marriage bond. The birth of children to a cohabiting couple, free to marry, was usually taken as prima facie evidence that they were in fact married, and could lead, *inter alia*, to parental obligation by both partners. Capacity to marry was important. Roman law set the minimum age for boys at 14, and for girls at 12, though there was a preference that both partners should already have reached puberty before marriage, and this generally meant 14 for girls at that time. Both partners had to be judged capable of making free consent. Consanguinity was avoided and rules limiting choice in class, race and citizenship were strictly applied, as was consent by the bride's father.

47.   Thus described, the institution of marriage in the world of the early Christians might seem more ordered than it actually was, and of course the situation was continually changing and was in any case diversely affected by local customs. The Roman satirists, however, do not tell the whole story and happy, enduring marriage was not unfamiliar to the ancient world.

48.   Since Jewish weddings were informal home-based affairs, and, notwithstanding their serious religious context, not conducted by a Rabbi until after the seventh century AD, Judaism could offer no distinctive liturgy of marriage which the Christians could copy or adapt. But much more important, there was in Judaism the long tradition of the so-called Noachian Commandments, that is the seven precepts which the Rabbis attributed, in their commentaries on the book of Genesis, to the time of Noah; the argument was that, since all mankind descended from Noah but the Gentiles could not be expected to observe the Jewish law, God had provided for them these minimal precepts

which served as a kind of Natural Law for all peoples and races. Among these precepts was the avoiding of incest, which the Rabbis interpreted as having a wide meaning, to exclude all forms of sexual irregularity outside marriage.

49. The earliest Christians, largely of Jewish origin as they were, would have been familiar with this Rabbinic tradition, and before their conversion would have seen it applied to the Gentiles in their midst. It is clear from, for example, the record of the Apostolic decrees of the Council of Jerusalem (Acts 15.28–29) and from similar passages in St Paul's Epistles that the early Church used the Noachian precepts as occasion demanded, to provide a basic moral outline for Gentile converts, and indeed also for converts from Judaism who need no longer feel bound by the Torah in its complexity and detail. In particular, for marriage, family life and sexual activity, the precepts provided a basic guideline for Jews and Gentiles alike. Indeed, in view of the sayings of Jesus himself about marriage recorded in the Gospels, and the respect shown in the early Church for Old Testament scripture, it could hardly have been otherwise. For the first two Christian centuries the task was to teach and encourage the followers of Christ to conform their marriages to God's original design, described in the book of Genesis and reiterated by the Lord himself.

50. Given the scattered and somewhat vulnerable nature of the earliest Christian communities, leaders of the Christian Church had no choice but to accept the prevailing laws and customs of the region. Converts already married were treated as such and asked to conform to Christian teachings about their relationship. Those already baptised and wishing to marry were encouraged to select Christian partners and, after the completion of the civil ceremonies required by law and custom, were invited to share with the local congregation in the Eucharist and offer their union to the Lord for his blessing. Apart from the emphasis on permanence and chastity within the marriage, the Christian teaching was distinct with regard to widows, in a world where many relatively young women found themselves alone again after a few years of marriage; whereas Roman custom encouraged them to remarry as soon as possible, keeping to the single state was commended among the Christians, comparable with the emerging emphasis on virginity.

51. Among the Fathers of the Church, Ignatius of Antioch (in his Epistle to Polycarp) and Tertullian stress the role of the local minister or bishop in approving the proposed union that it may be done 'after the

Lord, and to the honour of God', and there are early signs here of ecclesiastical supervision. Towards the end of the second century AD, ascetic and Montanist tendencies in the Church tended to stress exclusive and distinct forms of marriage for Christians and, to rebut these, Clement of Alexandria and other apologists affirm the recognition of marriage as part of God's universal provision for mankind. Evidence for Baptism and Communion after civil marriages can be matched by a more homely pattern in which the local bishop joined in the domestic ceremonies as an honoured guest, not dissimilar from our Lord's presence at the Cana wedding. It is probably the case that Christian Baptism was seen as a replacement for the pagan ritual marriage bath, and the Eucharist came to take the place of the sacred meal or cake provided by the religious official in old Roman practice, but it has to be noted that all this early and often conflicting evidence for the Christian marriage tradition is fragmentary and local. There was no universal system, and the references we have occur *en passant* amidst controversies about the virtues of virginity for all Christians, celibacy for the clergy, and general discouragement of adultery and divorce. It is from the oldest liturgies, and to some extent from decisions by Councils of the Church, that the standard pattern of marriage for Christians can be best identified, as that gradually becomes, especially after Constantine, the predominant European pattern.

52.   From Constantine to Charlemagne, five turbulent centuries, as the power and particularly the jurisdiction of the Church in matrimonial matters gradually extended through Europe, the Canon law, based largely on codification of increasingly Christianised versions of the old Roman law, came to predominate, at least officially. Free consent in public before witnesses by those having capacity was the essential norm, and the local priest came to be regarded as the reliable official who could ascertain that the intending partners were of age, outside the prohibited degrees of affinity, and capable of consent. However, throughout this period and later, the Church's claim to exclusive control was continually disputed and the old local laws, particularly in Northern Europe, proved tenacious. This official system co-existed in many places alongside local customary law, and marriages were recognised even when technically irregular, since it was in no one's interest to destroy partnerships that were obviously permanent, or unnecessarily to declare children illegitimate.

53.   That said, the trend was irrevocably set towards a crucial distinction between spiritual matters, the realm of the Church, and temporal

matters, the realm of the King, and somewhere between the tenth and twelfth centuries, as scholars now recognise, the logic of this distinction was applied progressively in European states by the creation of ecclesiastical courts who took over jurisdiction, in spiritual matters, from the secular courts.

54.   It may surprise some readers of this Report that the Christian attitude to marriage, clear as it has been from the beginning, should have gained such an established position in Europe only after some twelve hundred years. This may be partly accounted for by a supposition that the ideals of Christendom were practised for many centuries before; in fact, they gained ascendancy as the culmination of a long process. In so far as they did, it was the result of Christian determination to press its moral teaching on all who would listen and of the attempts made to discipline church members. It may be supposed that the substantial evidence of wedding services being held in church implies that in past times most, if not all, citizens were married in this way. Social history does not indicate such uniformity.

55.   The early liturgies for marriage, dating from the fifth century, are only available in fragments, but in the Leonine Sacramentary, based on these, provision is made for a Nuptial Mass which includes a blessing of the newly wed couple. This pattern has persisted ever since and occurs in the present day Order of the Roman Catholic Church. In parenthesis it can be noted that, in England, the influential Sarum rite provided for a Mass to follow the wedding ceremony, and in the first English Prayer Books of 1549 and 1552 the couple are told they must receive Communion the same day. The more familiar Prayer Book of 1662, emerging from a century of controversy, has the rubric 'It is convenient that the new-married persons should receive the holy Communion at the time of their Marriage, or at the first opportunity after their marriage.' The 1928 revision retained this rubric and made provision for Holy Communion following the wedding service, and in the Alternative Service Book of 1980 provision is made for alternative marriage services, with or without Holy Communion.

Marriage in England

56.   In some respects the English experience has been similar to that of Europe generally, but in others it has been understandably distinct. Long before the Norman Conquest, the Church in England exercised a ministry to those seeking marriage alongside and competing with the customary pattern of Saxon times. Until the eleventh century these

well-established conventions included polygamy, concubinage and easy 'divorce'. In the eyes of the laity of those times, marriage often seemed to be a private contract, either between two families, involving the settlement of property, or between two individuals, enforced largely by the community sense of what was 'right'.

57.　When Lanfranc, the Norman, was brought over by the Conqueror to be Archbishop of Canterbury, his zeal for reforming the ways of the English Church included not only the imposition of some further parts of the rapidly developing western Canon law, but also an unsuccessful attempt to insist, though the Canons did not, that valid marriage depended on the presence of a priest. Very frequently a priest might assist, and his presence would be valuable evidence, in the absence of written records, that a marriage had taken place, but the rule held that consent before witnesses made the marriage. So the newly established ecclesiastical courts recognised the doctrine that mutual consent was the essence of validity. Pragmatically they had little choice. As Moorman[1] and others have shown, the old customs of arranged marriages and private troth-plighting, possibly followed by a church ceremony when the wife was proved to be pregnant, persisted whatever the bishops and their officers might require.

58.　The church ceremony, moreover, did not always include the Nuptial Mass. Chaucer has his Wife of Bath declare that she was properly married six times at the church door, as indeed she was, as there was no legal requirement to enter the building. Only in the 1549 Prayer Book was the requirement made that on the day appointed for the solemnisation of the marriage, the persons to be married should come *into the body of the church* with their friends and neighbours.

59.　The Church's effective control of the ceremonies of marriage remained far from general, even into the nineteenth century, though the jurisdiction of the ecclesiastical courts, acting on the principles of monogamy and indissolubility, remained in force. Moreover, although matrimonial matters lay within the realm of the ecclesiastical courts, the all-important and inextricably associated jurisdiction in property matters lay in the secular courts; and, in such regulation of property law, a marriage would sometimes be presumed to subsist, even if only contracted by the procedures of custom.

---

[1] *Church Life in the Thirteenth Century*, J. R. H. Moorman, CUP 1945. For works consulted in the preparation of this chapter see Appendix 6.

60.   Certainly in the sixteenth century, although there seems to have
been an accepted understanding of what constituted the married state,
there were still a number of ways of entering it, recognised and accepted
within the communities in which a couple lived. There remained a
marked distinction between the necessary public steps to a marriage
where property was involved and the more private domestic arrangements of the unpropertied classes. The espousal or betrothal followed
by consummation was as much a marriage in the eyes of the courts as
any subsequent church ceremony. In many areas a binding agreement
between the parties in the face of witnesses sufficed for a marriage
recognised by all concerned, including, in practice, the local church,
provided no ecclesiastical offence was alleged.

61.   In the sixteenth and seventeenth centuries, there were well-
known and regulated forms for public weddings in families with
property. Banns were called, and surrounding the church rite there
were a good many social customs, the correct and exact observance of
which was of great significance in popular estimation. The importance
of betrothal and the customs surrounding the taking of the bride from
her parental home, leading to the establishment of a new household,
reflected the significant social consequences of marriage in the life of the
local community. Although the church rite was an element in such
public nuptial celebrations, it was by no means always regarded by the
participants as the most important, and there are many accounts which
suggest that customs surrounding the giving of the ring and other
tokens and the taking of the bridal garter (which took place during the
church ceremony) were often regarded by guests and witnesses–
sometimes even by the officiating priest–as carrying more significance
than the liturgical action.

62.   Such public marriages had marked social and economic
consequences and were widely publicised events. They were not over-
frequent, for the scope for establishment of new households in relatively
static economic conditions was limited. There were also ways in which
those unable to fulfil the economic and social demands of a public
wedding could regulate their conjugal relations. The expedient
recounted in Shakespeare's *Romeo and Juliet*, in which family
expectations were bypassed by the couple resorting privately to an
unbeneficed priest (Friar Lawrence) reflected a practice which would
have been known and recognised by the play's original audiences.
Marriage by any priest would have been regarded as valid marriage and
sufficient sanction for conjugal relations and legitimate status for

children of the union. Such private marriage would, however, have been popularly regarded in quite a different light from a public wedding. Though private ceremony avoided the economic and social consequence of establishing a new household, it would not be likely to withstand social pressures which would enforce separation if the parents could not be persuaded to recognise a *fait accompli* or if a poorer couple, thus wed, fell on hard times and became chargeable to the parish. Private weddings, and the Church's blessing of them, were unpopular with the propertied (and Puritan) classes. Moreover, the possibility of a private wedding encouraged irresponsible action by some clergy, so that the commerce in 'Fleet' weddings (conducted by unscrupulous clergy in places which were effectively exempt from any ecclesiastical control) became notorious.

63. Any wedding contracted by liturgical rite and witnessed by a priest would, of course, have been recognised by the Church as canonically binding. A further possibility was the widespread recognition given to a couple who had contracted a union by recognised and socially accepted betrothal customs but without church rite. When such unions resulted in pregnancy there would often be a marriage by church rite, but this was by no means always so, since there seems to have been a general social and legal acceptance of the legitimacy of such unions. There were strong pressures in public policy – not resisted by the Church – to accept and recognise a stable union as a marriage, and its offspring as legitimate, wherever possible.

64. As the corollary to this social acceptance of more or less private unions there is widespread evidence of 'divorce' and subsequent 'remarriage' by a variety of recognised folk-customs. 'Wife sale' was, perhaps, the most prevalent of these, being available to the lower classes. In such cases the 'purchaser' was often known to the husband, the 'sale' being but the public enactment of a previously concluded agreement.

65. Before the mid-eighteenth century, therefore, marriage could be entered by a 'bewildering variety of ways'.[1] The present-day difficulty for some people, of deciding whether a civil wedding could be described as true marriage, is more than paralleled by the difficulties of defining what was and what was not marriage in the period before

---

[1] *The Family, Sex and Marriage in England 1500-1800*, L. Stone, Penguin 1979, p.29

1753. The Church's requirements for marriage were but one element (even though a powerful influence) in the complexity of social custom and folklore which operated in such matters.

66. Perhaps the focal point for an understanding of the history of marriage in England and Wales is Lord Hardwicke's Marriage Act of 1753. After its enactment, until 1836, the only legally recognised entry into the married state, except for Jews and Quakers, was by the marriage ceremony of the Church of England. More is said about this Act in the following chapter (para. 92).

67. The requirements of the 1753 Act, followed closely afterwards by the social upheaval occasioned by the industrial revolution and the absence, until the 1830s, of effective central registration would all appear to be contributory factors in the marked growth in recorded cohabitation and illegitimacy. Recent research suggests that in some places between ten and fifteen per cent of the population was illegitimate at the end of the eighteenth and beginning of the nineteenth century. It is possible to interpret such trends as a continuation of the distinction between public and private marriage, with the difference that the 1753 Act deterred some of those entering into more private relationships from seeking ministrations of the Church. In earlier years, people who were unable to fulfil the social requirements of a public wedding had resorted to an unbeneficed priest for the solemnisation of their union. After 1753 this possibility was no longer open to them. In the circumstances of the time, the requirement of banns and the expense of a licence were, for some people, disincentives to marriage in the parish church.

68. It is not easy to substantiate these assertions beyond dispute, given the limitations of the available evidence (of necessity only arising from that small proportion of private conjugal arrangements which, for one reason or another, came to public attention). There is, however, consistent testimony from such records as do exist that, despite the omission of a registered marriage ceremony, many such unions were entered into before witnesses, and were expressions of a serious intent to live in a stable union. One effect of the 1753 Act was, therefore, to distance the Church from more private traditions of entering the married state at a period when social and economic pressures were making such private arrangements more frequent in the newly industrialised conurbations.

69. 'Common-law' liaisons survived longest amongst the lowest social classes and in boom towns where the social framework was less

fixed. There is some nineteenth-century evidence to suggest that the aspect of the older folk customs which survived longest was that which sanctioned unofficial 'divorce' and 'remarriage' since dissolution of a marriage remained an expensive and inconvenient remedy to obtain for all but an affluent minority of the population. After approximately 1850, however, there were developments which served to restore marriage to a more central place in most people's experience. It is these developments which give rise to the current tradition of the 'white' wedding in church as an aspiration for many couples from all sections of society.

70.   Complex social and economic changes enhanced the status of married 'respectability', and severely restricted the acceptability of less regulated domestic arrangements. These social and economic changes included *(a)* the greater efficiency of central registration after 1836, *(b)* the diminished isolation of local communities in a period of increased mobility and communication, *(c)* changes in the administration of the poor law after 1834 (which lessened the possibilities of out-relief and tended towards a harsher treatment of illegitimate offspring, even though making affiliation orders available to the mother for the first time), and *(d)* the displacement of much independent family-based economy by wage-earning employment in large manufactories whose owners were increasingly inclined, in a changing moral climate, to stigmatise and discriminate against those whose lifestyle varied from middle-class expectations. The cumulative effect of these pressures was such that by the end of the nineteenth century married 'respectability' was more necessary for almost all the poorer classes, particularly women, than had been the case throughout the preceding centuries. The evidence of social historians seems to suggest, however, that it was by economic pressures, rather than ethical convictions, that the change was effected. It thus became important, as never before, for a working-class marriage to be open and public, to demonstrate its conformity to conventional standards. It is possible to argue that modification of those standards in recent decades has allowed a re-emergence of earlier attitudes rather than caused any fundamental change.

71.   The preceding paragraphs are no more than an outline of the complexities of the historical background to our present situation, and it must be emphasised that arguments from historical precedent do not provide neat answers to present-day problems. Nonetheless, a realistic appreciation of the prevailing circumstances, and of reactions to them,

in other centuries is essential to understand the current situation and its implications for the present-day Church.

II INTERNATIONAL PERSPECTIVES: MARRIAGE OUTSIDE ENGLAND

72.   Part of our assessment of the past has been an appreciation of the variety of historical circumstances which have led to the development of different practices and customs in other places, particularly in other parts of the British Isles and on the mainland of Europe.

73.   There is first the need to describe, very briefly, the position in Wales, Scotland and Northern Ireland. It is not always realised that their practice is not the same as in England.

Wales

74.   Until 1919 the Church in Wales was established and the legal position, including the place within it of the Church, was exactly as in England. Since disestablishment, the Church in Wales continues to enjoy a privileged position under the Marriage Acts 1949 to 1986. Except that only members of the Church in Wales may bring complaints before the Welsh ecclesiastical courts, there is little difference between the position of the Church in Wales and that of the Church of England in relation to the Canon law of marriage. However, a minister of the Church in Wales is in a stronger position to refuse to marry a person where the refusal is not covered by a specific statutory provision, for example that relating to divorced people. Should an incumbent in Wales refuse to marry a person on the grounds that he or she was unbaptised, only members of the Church in Wales would be able to bring a complaint against the incumbent in the Provincial Court.

Scotland

75.   The present legal position in Scotland is quite different from that in England, and this is the result of a markedly different historical development, until 1707 within a separate kingdom. The phenomenon of 'Gretna Green' is the most widely known facet of that difference. The 1753 Act did not apply in Scotland, and customs akin to the earlier situation in England (though with distinctive Scottish features) continued to exist. The current position (since 1977) is that, for regular marriage, preliminary notice of intention to marry is submitted to the district registrar who, after not less than 14 days, issues a notice specifying the date and place of the marriage's solemnisation. This procedure applies to all marriages, civil or religious (of any

denomination). A further difference between Scottish and English practice is that irregular marriages may still be constituted, in law, by cohabitation with habit and repute 'for a considerable time' (usually at least three years). Since such marriages do not involve a ceremony, the question of the Church's involvement in this does not formally arise. Although the Church of Scotland has an 'established' position, decisions as to who may or may not marry in its churches (i.e. whether baptised or not) are determined by the Church courts, and that Church's binding obligation to resident parishioners has been modified since the introduction of universal civil preliminaries in 1977.

Northern Ireland

76.   In Northern Ireland the position is complex and differs according to the denominational setting within which the marriage is to take place. Civil marriage is available on the same basis as in England. For a religious ceremony in the Church of Ireland, Presbyterian or Roman Catholic Churches, at least one partner must be a member of that denomination (and if banns are to be called, both must be).

Other European Countries

77.   There is reference in Canon Rhymes's motion (forming the second strand in the Group's terms of reference) to universal civil marriage. That system is frequently described, and has been referred to as such in evidence given to us, as the Continental system. We must dispel any illusion that there is, elsewhere in Europe, a uniform system of civil marriage, which might or might not be followed by a religious ceremony depending on the couple's religious convictions and commitment. We have been at some pains to hear of the practice of the other countries of Western Europe and the Commonwealth and of the USA. It is clear that there is a great variety in practice. The current position in each country has evolved from particular circumstances of history and culture, though the Christian tradition has been a consistently strong influence in all such developments wherever the Christian faith has been the prevailing religious belief.

78.   All present-day European states have come to provide a civil ceremony for those not wishing to marry by religious rite. Apart from this common feature, there are several 'patterns' in use.

'Established Church'

79.   An 'English' system operates in the Scandinavian countries – where the ecclesiastical parish remains as the primary unit for civil registration.

Anyone in Denmark, Sweden, Norway, Finland or Iceland, whether baptised or not, is deemed to be a member of the national Church unless a positive disclaimer is made, and may be married in the parish church. There is also freedom to be married by the rites of some other recognised denominations.

Entrenched Church Role

80.   In Italy, Spain and Portugal a broadly similar right exists, with the important proviso that a Church wedding is not available if neither party is baptised or if either is divorced. In Greece the proviso as to Baptism applies but, in accordance with Orthodox practice, second and third (but not later) marriages can be conducted by Church rite (after either death or divorce).

Universal Civil Marriage

81.   In France, Belgium, the Netherlands, West Germany and Austria there is universal civil marriage. This may, at the couple's choice, be followed by a religious ceremony. For Roman Catholics, this is regarded as obligatory and would be seen by the couple to be the 'real' wedding; for Protestants the church ceremony, although very frequent, would generally speaking be regarded as additional. A Protestant Church would not question the effectiveness of the civil ceremony in establishing the marriage, although a subsequent religious service might include an exchange of vows.

82.   In those countries where universal civil marriage is required it has been the civil authority, not the Church, which has initiated the requirement. In the anti-religious fervour of the French Revolution it was introduced in France and spread widely in Europe under the influence of the Code Napoleon; after 1815 it was retained in France and the Low Countries. In some Protestant states of Germany, from the sixteenth century, the tradition had been for the marriage to be made by consent before (optional) rites in church. This practice, far from being secular, sprang out of a profoundly religious conviction of the complementarity of Church and State (not far removed from that which informed public policy in our own sixteenth- and seventeenth-century history); by the eighteenth century, however, the church ceremony had become general. After the unification of Germany, Bismarck's policy of *Kulturkampf* introduced universal civil marriage throughout the unified German Empire, primarily as an anti-Catholic policy.

Non-Christian Influence

83. The prevalence of universal civil marriage in Europe has been extended by the advent of Communism. Eastern Europe, whether the predominant Christian tradition is Orthodox, Roman Catholic or Protestant, now requires civil marriage, whatever Church rite might follow.

84. The degree of anti-clericalism and militant secularism shown by the civil authorities and in the general population also affects the position. In France there is often a clear-cut distinction between Church families and anti-clerical, non-Church families. Even there, however, there are in many places strong pressures, in practice difficult to resist, to provide a religious ceremony after civil marriage even for the most 'nominal' of Roman Catholics (and there has been some informal experimentation with services of prayer after the civil marriage of divorced people). In Belgium, on the other hand, despite formal separation of Church and State, the overwhelming Catholic ethos puts on to the Roman Catholic Church many of the pressures and problems experienced in the Church of England. There are many infant Baptisms of children of non-practising parents, with the purpose of securing for such children the opportunity of a church wedding.

85. The impact of non-Christian faiths in Europe is also being felt. Where civil marriage is required of all, some members of other faiths wish for a religious rite after the bare and minimal civil ceremony. The Christian Church sometimes becomes involved. We have learned, for instance, of some Churches in Belgium being approached by Japanese non-Christians for a form of religious service (not the Roman Catholic marriage rite).

Commonwealth Countries

86. The marriage practice in Commonwealth countries, although for the most part developing from the English system, differs from it in that in no Commonwealth country does the Anglican Church have responsibilities to all citizens which can be claimed as of right. In Australia and New Zealand, for example, there exists the choice between civil or religious ceremony in accordance with any recognised religious rite and any such religious body, including the Anglican Church, is free to decline to marry applicants to whom it does not wish to minister. In other Commonwealth countries, for example Nigeria (where there are Muslim and tribal customs to accommodate), there is universal civil marriage as understood in France or Belgium.

United States of America

87.   In the USA the Federal law provides the framework for essential elements in a marriage; State law is responsible for the development and application of the law of marriage in each State. In every State a couple must apply in person to the civil authority for a Marriage Licence which will be granted when the State's requirements have been met (e.g. interview and/or medical examination). The couple may take their Licence either to a civic representative (usually a justice of the peace or judge) or to a clergyman who is registered with the State and holds a Licence to represent the State in performing marriage. The venue for the ceremony is entirely at the choice of the couple or the convenience of the officiant. If a clergyman acts, he or she signs the Marriage Licence, as do the couple, and it is returned to the civil authorities and serves as the official registration of the marriage.

Implications of the Practice of other Churches and in other States

88.   It is apparent, even from this brief survey of marriage practice outside England, that there is diversity of practice and approach and even where the Church is distanced from the legally recognised ceremony there is not necessarily a diminution of requests for marriage from those who give only a nominal allegiance to the Church. We have heard evidence that in England the Free Churches, and particularly the Roman Catholic Church, are often under very strong pressure to accede to requests for marriage that are made to them, even where there is little evidence of religious commitment. The same is true elsewhere in Europe and in the Commonwealth countries. There are bound to be many, whose commitment to the Christian faith is nominal, who will, nevertheless, seek out the Church for their wedding and who, therefore, have some claim on the pastoral care offered by the Church. Those who advocate universal civil marriage, or a discretion for English clergy to decline to marry their parishioners in certain circumstances, need to take note of these circumstances.

CHAPTER 3

The Law of Marriage and Divorce in England

89.   The 'Law of Marriage' can be discerned by examining (a) the law relating to the contracting of marriages, (b) the law relating to the dissolution of marriages and (c) the law as it applies to those who are in the married state.

THE DEVELOPMENT OF THE LAW

90.   The medieval common law was primarily concerned with marriage as giving rise to property rights: for example, a widow would be entitled to dower only if she could establish that she had been married, and a son could inherit only if he was legitimate (which would depend on whether his parents had been married). If there was doubt about the existence or validity of the marriage, the common law courts would refer the question to the ecclesiastical courts and accept their judgment. As the *Tametsi* decree of the Council of Trent of 1563 (which, in order to prevent clandestine marriages, required a marriage to be contracted in the presence of a priest and two or three witnesses) did not apply in this country, the English ecclesiastical courts continued to apply the old doctrine that no formalities were required for the solemnisation of a marriage.

91.   Although there were some voices at the time of the Reformation which suggested that the legal contracting of marriages was not the proper business of the Church, in England the Protestant settlement made no changes to the received understanding of the role of the Church in English society. Indeed, Hooker's view of the establishment – of the Church as one aspect of the one society – only served to give further justification for the continued role of the Church in these matters.

92.   The fact that an informal marriage was perfectly valid in law was a matter of grave concern. A marriage, which one of the parties believed to be valid, might turn out to be a nullity because the other had previously contracted an informal union. At common law, marriage

29

vested most of the wife's property in the husband and the ease with which an informal marriage could be contracted meant that a rich heiress presented a valuable catch to an unscrupulous rogue. A number of scandals in the first half of the eighteenth century led to the passing of Lord Hardwicke's Marriage Act in 1753 to prevent these clandestine marriages. Unless a special licence had been obtained, a marriage had to be solemnised in the parish church of the parish in which one of the parties resided after the publication of banns or the issue of a common licence. Any marriage not in accordance with these provisions would be void. (The only exceptions to the general rule related to marriages according to the usages of the Society of Friends and marriages according to Jewish rites provided that both parties were Quakers or Jews respectively.)

93. The Hardwicke Act established the pattern for the conduct of marriages in modern times. It brought to the surface, however, another persistent problem which related to the failure of the 1662 settlement to unite the Christian Church in England. The Act required Dissenters to marry in their parish church according to the rites of the Church of England. In addition, the needs of the small residual English Roman Catholic community were not covered by the Act. The repeal of the Test and Corporation Acts (1828) and the Catholic Emancipation Act (1829) marked a major step in removing social and political disabilities on Dissenters and Roman Catholics. There were still those, such as the Unitarians, who felt their consciences to be under unreasonable pressure because of the references to the Trinity in the marriage service and those who, as ministers or members of other Churches, resented the need for all marriages to be conducted by Anglican clergy according to Anglican rites.

94. Two important Acts of Parliament were passed in 1836. The first was the Marriage Act, which had two purposes:

(*a*) to permit a superintendent registrar of marriages to issue a certificate entitling the persons named on it to marry each other. It was originally intended that this should be obligatory for marriages in the Church of England too, but ecclesiastical opposition to this proposal was too great.

(*b*) to enable those who so wished to contract a marriage in a building registered for religious worship 'according to such form and ceremony as they may wish to adopt' or to contract a marriage in a register office in the presence of the superintendent registrar with no religious ceremony at all.

This Act thus defused grievances felt by non-Anglicans.

95.   The second Act passed in 1836 was the Registration Act. This sought to establish a more efficient system of registering births and deaths as well as marriages. Criticism had been expressed about the efficiency of the clergy of the established Church in registering marriages, and this Act seemed to cause them more concern than the Marriage Act.

96.   One further important change in the law should be mentioned. Under the Act of 1836 a registrar had to be present at a marriage conducted in a registered building, but the Marriage Act of 1898 permitted the trustees of such a building to appoint an 'authorised person' (who will normally be a minister of the particular denomination) before whom a marriage can be solemnised without the need for a registrar to be present. These Acts established the basic position as it is today.

97.   It is widely held that, by providing that virtually all marriages should be solemnised in the Church of England, Lord Hardwicke's Act gave everyone the legal right to be married in his or her parish church (except perhaps if both parties were Quakers or Jews). The present position is obscure and will probably remain so: an aggrieved parishioner is unlikely to take proceedings to test the legality of an incumbent's refusal to permit him to marry in his church. Although it has been possible to contract a marriage otherwise than according to Anglican rites since 1836, most authorities nevertheless agree that a parishioner still has the right to be married in his or her parish church. The argument is developed more fully in Appendix 1.

THE POSITION TODAY

98.   After 1836 there was a slow and steady increase in the number of marriages contracted outside the Church of England. In 1845 out of a total of 143,743 marriages the number conducted by the Church of England was 129,515 (90 per cent). In 1986 out of 347,924 marriages 117,804 were conducted by the Churches of England and Wales (34 per cent).

99.   There was no suggestion in any of this that the meaning of the institution of marriage, which people entered by one or other of these means, varied according to the route the couple chose for themselves.

The understanding of the institution of marriage is common in English law. There is no such thing as one sort of marriage conducted in the established Church and a different sort of marriage conducted in the register office.

100.   This common understanding of the nature of marriage in English law was described by Lord Penzance in the case of *Hyde v. Hyde* in 1866 in the following words:

> I conceive that marriage, as understood in Christendom, may . . . be defined as the voluntary union for life of one man and one woman to the exclusion of all others.

The parties (who must have the legal capacity to marry each other) must freely consent to entering into a heterosexual and monogamous partnership. According to the tradition of the Western Church, marriage was rightly described as a union for life. The Church of England retained this doctrine after the Reformation and until recently the Church and the law unquestioningly accepted the same definition. In view of the large number of broken marriages, however, there is now an argument, not entirely cynical, for saying that marriage is for life unless it is dissolved by a decree of divorce. But marriage is still for life, even if terminable by divorce. It is not a state which can be entered with the intention that it should only last for a period of years or until some named eventuality.

101.   The legal position today is that a couple intending to enter into marriage in England or Wales must give notice to the appropriate officer. They must also take each other as husband and wife before witnesses, and the Marriage Acts lay down the place where, and the person before whom, the ceremony must take place.

(*a*) If the marriage is conducted according to the rites of the Church of England, it must normally take place in the parish church of the parish in which one of the parties resides (or in the church which is the usual place of worship of one of them) before a clerk in holy orders (who is also responsible for registering the marriage). It may also take place in any other building (for example, a college chapel) on the authority of a special licence issued on behalf of the Archbishop of Canterbury.

(*b*) A marriage may take place in a building certified as a place of religious worship which has been registered for the solemnisation of marriages. Any form of ceremony may be used, and the marriage must be conducted before an authorised person or a registrar.

(*c*) A purely civil ceremony may take place in a register office before a superintendent registrar and a registrar.

(d) Since 1983 it has also been possible for a house-bound or detained person to be married in the place where he or she is resident or is detained. (Both these terms have a limited meaning under the Marriage Act 1983.) Such a marriage may be purely civil in character or conducted in accordance with any religious ceremony (including rites of the Church of England).

DIVORCE AND THE LAW OF MARRIAGE

102.   There is nothing new about divorce. Even when marriage was the concern solely of the Church, it was possible for marriages to be dissolved by Act of Parliament. Private Acts were sought for this purpose from the reign of Charles II, and between 1715 and 1857 there were, on the average, one or two Parliamentary divorces every year. Much of the background to the development of contemporary divorce law is set out in *Putting Asunder*, the 1966 report of the group appointed by the Archbishop of Canterbury to consider the law of divorce. Appendix A of that report sets out the essential history of the development of the law of divorce up to 1966 and the way the Church reacted to these developments.

103.   For our purposes it is necessary to take note of the points of similarity between the issues with which this Report is concerned and those raised at crucial periods in the past. Having provided for marriage by ceremonies other than those of the Church of England, Parliament turned its attention to the needs of those seeking divorce. The debate on this question, which began in 1854, bears a striking similarity to those subsequently conducted in the Church on the same subject. There were those like the Bishop of St David's (Connop Thirlwall) and F. D. Maurice who noted that the respective functions of Church and State in these matters might not be the same. John Keble noted that the passing of such a law would mean that state matrimonial law would differ from the rule of the Church. Such legislation, whilst appropriate for those who owed no loyalty to the Church, should not override the provisions of the Book of Common Prayer and the Canons.

104.   The 1857 Act placed the clergy of the Church of England in a new and potentially difficult position. As they were now under an obligation to conduct marriages for all residents in the parish who were legally entitled to be married they might now be confronted with a request to conduct the marriages of divorced persons whose previous marital partners were still living. The 1857 Act relieved clergymen of

the Church of England from the duty to solemnise the marriage of a person who had been divorced on the ground of his or her own adultery, but they were bound to solemnise the marriage of the innocent party (even though his or her former spouse was still alive). Furthermore, an incumbent refusing to conduct a marriage service because one of the parties had been divorced for adultery had to permit his church to be used for this purpose if another clergyman was willing to perform the ceremony. It was not until the Matrimonial Causes Act of 1937 extended the grounds for divorce to include cruelty, desertion and incurable insanity that a clergyman was relieved from the obligation to solemnise the marriage of *any* divorced person during the lifetime of his or her former spouse or to permit the use of his church or chapel for this purpose.[1]

105. The pressure for further reform of the law of divorce grew during the post-1945 period. The war had taken its toll of many marriages. Irrespective of social position in Britain, there were many couples who did not succeed in re-establishing their marriages after the separation caused by the demands of military and other public service during the war. The resulting demand for divorce, coupled with the establishment of legal aid in 1949 (which, following wartime provision by the Law Society to help members of the Forces, enabled many more people to petition for divorce), led to a marked increase in the number of decrees. Even after the direct impact of the war had worked its way through the post-1945 peak, there was a steady underlying increase of demand for divorce. The number of petitions filed moved upwards from 32,000 in 1961 to 47,000 in 1966. Alongside this was the expression of discontent among lawyers and the public alike at a law based on the concept of matrimonial offence. The offence appeared all too often to be the result or the symptom of the breakdown of the marriage rather than its cause. The courts were being asked to decide on guilt and innocence in a situation involving the complexities of human relationships. The appearance (and subsequent withdrawal) of Mrs Eirene White's Bill to permit divorce on the grounds of seven years' separation indicated public concern. The report of the Royal Commission, set up in 1957 to consider these matters, was unable to escape from the concept of matrimonial offence. In a minority statement, however, Lord Walker set out the case for substituting break-

---

[1] This provision was extended by the Marriage (Prohibited Degrees of Relationship) Act 1986 to marriages between parties related within certain degrees of affinity.

down for offence as the ground for divorce. In 1963 Mr Leo Abse took up where Mrs White had left off and sought to promote legislation for the reform of the law of divorce. Throughout, in a variety of ways, the Church had sought to make it clear that its predominant concern was that divorce law and procedure should be seen to uphold the institution of marriage. This is the background to the Archbishop of Canterbury's initiative in setting up the group under the chairmanship of the Rt Revd R. C. Mortimer, Bishop of Exeter, to consider divorce law.

106. *Putting Asunder* sought a framework for divorce law and procedure which would uphold the integrity of the institution of marriage as traditionally received in our history. There were two central features to its recommendations. First it propounded the concept of the 'irretrievable breakdown of marriage' as the sole legal ground for divorce. (*Putting Asunder* did not suggest that this meant that there was no fault in a divorce but that the ground for the law of divorce should be the irretrievable breakdown of marriage.) In this respect it was the first group formally set up by the Church of England to give public and theological support to this notion. *Putting Asunder* grasped the nettle of the implications for the law of divorce of the essentially relational factors in marriage breakdown. Second, it was clear in the mind of the authors that society, through the courts, had a duty to set up procedures which would ensure the proper demonstration of the irretrievable breakdown of a marriage, It did not accept that if a couple said their marriage had broken down irretrievably this should be sufficient for the granting of a divorce. There should, therefore, be a full and thorough judicial inquiry to establish to the satisfaction of the law that the marriage had broken down beyond retrieving. Such an inquiry would have to satisfy itself that all possibilities of reconciliation had been explored and were without reasonable hope of success. By such a procedure society would be demonstrating at one and the same time its desire for a humane law of divorce and its commitment to uphold and sustain the institution of marriage. In this respect it is worth quoting *Putting Asunder*, para. 69 (b), page 58:

> One of our reasons for recommending the principle of breakdown is that it would enable the courts to get to grips with the realities of the matrimonial relationship instead of having to concentrate on superficialities. But if the principle were introduced into the law in the shape of yet another verbally formulated 'ground'. . . the advantage hoped for would be lost. There would inevitably be a tendency simply to measure the circumstances revealed by the evidence against the verbal formula and, if they appeared to fit it and no bar applied, to grant a decree without any genuine trial of the issue of

breakdown. In other words, it is likely that the attitudes and procedures appropriate to the trial of matrimonial-offence cases would be extended to cases turning on the new 'ground'.

107.   *Putting Asunder* had more effect on the subsequent reform of the legal grounds for divorce than it had on the development of divorce law procedure. It was referred by the Lord Chancellor to the Law Commission. Their response, published in October 1966, agreed with *Putting Asunder* that the objectives of divorce law should be:

  (i) to buttress, rather than to undermine, the stability of marriage;
 (ii) when a marriage has irretrievably broken down to enable the empty legal shell to be destroyed with the maximum fairness, and the minimum bitterness, distress and humiliation.

They agreed that the sole ground for divorce should be the irretrievable breakdown of the marriage. However, they did not accept the need for a judicial inquiry. Crucial to *Putting Asunder*'s view was the commitment to a proper inquiry into the reasons for the divorce application. The Law Commission believed this to be impracticable in the light both of the demand on the time of the courts and of the experience of the courts in handling divorce cases under the old law. Their own proposals explicitly included elements of divorce by consent. After the debate of their report in the House of Lords, discussions took place between members of the Law Commission and the Archbishop's group, which led to the Divorce Reform Act 1969.

108.   The 1969 Act sought to find a practical route forward for a divorce law whose sole ground for divorce would be the irretrievable breakdown of the marriage. Instead of instituting a thorough inquiry into the breakdown of the marriage to prove the case, the Act established that the breakdown was to be proved by establishing one or more of five facts. These five facts are:

  (i) that the respondent has committed adultery and the petitioner finds it intolerable to live with the respondent;
 (ii) that the respondent has behaved in such a way that the petitioner cannot reasonably be expected to live with the respondent;
(iii) that the respondent has deserted the petitioner for a continuous period of two years;
 (iv) that the parties to the marriage have lived apart for two years and the respondent consents to the divorce;[1]
  (v) that the parties have lived apart for five years.

---

[1] This 'fact' was altered by the House of Lords–the Bill originally said 'does not object'; the House substituted 'consents'.

The court has a duty, as far as it is able, to inquire into the facts as alleged by the parties. If any of these facts is proved the court shall grant a decree (unless the breakdown appears not irretrievable).

109. The Act and the rules require a solicitor who acts for a party to certify whether he/she has discussed the possibility of reconciliation and provided names and addresses of people qualified to help. *Putting Asunder* wanted to make good use of the possibility which might exist for a reconciliation between the parties. It was not in favour of making recourse to such help compulsory. The legal provision, however, has no sanction attached to it. The solicitor is not, therefore, under any obligation to take action. He/she is not required to discuss the possibility of reconciliation nor is he/she required to supply names of persons qualified to help.

110. It was thought at the time by both Church and Parliament that a satisfactory outcome had been reached through these efforts. The Church had opened the way to a new definition of the ground for divorce. Agreement had been maintained on the need for divorce law both to provide an honest and humane end to marriages which had broken down beyond repair and to seek to uphold the dignity of the marriage contract. The Church had clearly recognised that there are distinct roles for Church and Parliament in these matters and that Parliament had a duty to make good provision for those who sought divorce. According to T. A. Lacey, in his book *Marriage in Church and State* (1912),

> It is the duty of a Christian to support the authority of the State. It may be his duty also to labour for the reformation of the laws of the State. In doing this he has no right to put aside what he has learnt as a Christian, and in the quality of citizenship to act as a mere natural man. Such a division of personality is intolerable. But neither is he bound to insist that the laws of the State, in regard to marriage or in regard to anything else, shall conform exactly to Christian teaching. Not all the subjects of the State are Christian, and the State must legislate for all. He is bound, however, to use his Christian illumination for ascertaining what is naturally just, and he is no less bound to ensue peace by endeavouring to bring the law into such a frame that it will not actually conflict with his obligations to the Church.

111. Subsequent experience of a rapid growth in the divorce rate, described in Chapter 4, together with further changes in divorce law and procedure, has led to a steady increase of concern in the Church that the outcome of the 1969 Act was, in fact, far from satisfactory.

112. The Matrimonial Causes Act of 1973 consolidated the provisions of the 1969 Act and the Matrimonial Proceedings and Property Act 1970. 1973 also saw the introduction of the special procedure. Originally this applied only to petitions based on two years' separation, but during the next four years it was extended and now applied to all undefended petitions for divorce and judicial separation (but not nullity); at the same time, entitlement to legal aid was virtually withdrawn for undefended petitions. Since the vast majority of cases (over 99 per cent) are undefended, the effect is that almost all divorce decrees are granted without either party attending the hearing and very often without any solicitor being involved. This is popularly regarded as divorce by post. We now effectively have the very thing that *Putting Asunder* specifically set its face against: divorce at the mere will of the parties. There are now less than 1,000 defended cases each year. If the suit is undefended, the court is virtually bound to accept that the marriage has irretrievably broken down if the petitioner states that he or she will not return to the respondent; consequently, if the petitioner can establish one or more of the five facts set out in the Act, the court must pronounce a decree. The position is exacerbated by the special procedure, which has deprived the court of the power of exercising its statutory duty to inquire into the facts alleged by the petitioner. It has thus made it easier for an unscrupulous spouse to obtain a decree based on false facts or an honest one to present a case which is so thin that it might well be dismissed if there were an oral hearing. But the special procedure may have had an even more subtle and profound effect by giving the impression that divorce is now obtainable on demand, at least if the other spouse declares his or her intention of not defending. If this is how the layman perceives the position, his belief (whether accurate or not) must necessarily affect his view of marriage as a lifelong union.

113. It is difficult, therefore, to escape the conclusion which Chancellor Bullimore came to in his booklet *Pushing Asunder?* (Grove Books 1981), p.16:

> The Church must take a large share of credit, and responsibility, for making irretrievable breakdown the basis of our law of divorce. The Archbishop's Group however did not see what a chasm was opening up for their overall aims in agreeing to abandon the necessity for an inquiry into each marriage. Perhaps even the distinguished lawyers in the group did not do so. The result was that even though the rules changed and the object of the exercise changed, in practice, we have the same dog on a different piece of string. All that can be said in the end, is that irretrievable breakdown is a better criterion for divorce than the matrimonial offence. The report itself cannot

be thought, as it became law, to have achieved in any way that which all the members of the Group endorsed, the bolstering of the institution of marriage itself. Divorce law turns out to be about ending marriages and in no sense saving or protecting them. Could it be otherwise? Those who desire to strengthen marriage and family life at this point are clearly too late.

114.   The Church's growing concern in these matters has been further added to by the 1984 Matrimonial Causes and Family Proceedings Act. The main expressed anxiety of the Church with this legislation concerned its reduction of the time restriction on couples for the presentation of petitions for divorce. Before this Act there was a three-year time bar after the contracting of the marriage, It was possible for couples to seek a divorce during these three years but only on the ground of the exceptional hardship to the petitioner or the exceptional depravity of the respondent. The view of the Law Commission was set out in its Working Paper 76 and confirmed in its final report, Paper 112, laid before Parliament in 1982. Briefly, it suggested, among other things, that the time restriction be reduced to one year with no exception. The concern of the Church of England was expressed by the Board for Social Responsibility on a number of occasions, including the giving of oral evidence to the Special Standing Committee of the House of Commons set up to examine the Bill. It was felt by the Board that, in the context of the special procedure, this proposal would only serve to increase the recourse of couples to divorce proceedings as the only way of seeking relief for their marital distress. Unless the procedure for divorce were reformed to enable the needs of couples to be more fully met, such a change would only serve to add to the already growing impression that the law of divorce was undermining the stability of the institution of marriage. It was this point which the Board reiterated in its response to the Booth Committee Green Paper:

> The State has a proper interest in the stability of marriage. This is not merely a private relationship between two persons but also a public institution in which society has an interest (*Marriage, Divorce and the Church*, SPCK 1971, p.98 f.). In every register office in the land there is a notice to the effect that, according to the laws of the realm, marriage is a voluntary union of one man and one woman for life. Although the law properly enables relief to be given to couples in cases where the marriage has irretrievably broken down, it is important that the procedures which give this relief should uphold, or at any rate should not undermine, marriage as an institution which people who undertake it intend to be permanent.[1]

---

[1] The Response of the Board for Social Responsibility to the Matrimonial Causes Procedure Committee of the Lord Chancellor's Department, February 1984, p.1

115. The progress through Parliament of the Matrimonial and Family Proceedings Bill took place at the same time as the Church of England General Synod was wrestling with the problem of the discipline of the Church over the remarriage of divorced persons in church. It was in the context of these debates and in the light of the Board for Social Responsibility's comments (set out in GS Misc. 173, *Time Restrictions on Presentation of Divorce and Nullity Petitions*, June 1983) that some members of Synod and others expressed concern about the state of the law of marriage and divorce and the perceived distance between this and the Church's view of marriage.

116. It is not only the Church which has expressed concern about the present state of the law and procedure. There has been growing concern among lawyers about the need for improved provision in this area. The establishment and growth of the Family Law Association in recent years is an example of such concern. Similarly, at an official level, there continues to be a comprehensive review of the law and procedure in the area of matrimonial and family law. The Lord Chancellor's Department and the Law Commission have been looking at all areas of legal provision in these matters. Three particular areas which relate to our concerns–procedure, conciliation, and the ground and the facts–have been under review.

Procedure

117. The first area is procedure. In September 1982 the Lord Chancellor set up a Committee under the Chairmanship of the Hon. Mrs Justice Booth OBE with the following terms of reference:

> To examine the procedure and practice of the High Court and County Courts in respect of proceedings under the Matrimonial Causes Act 1973, and to recommend reforms which might be made:
> (*a*) to mitigate the intensity of disputes;
> (*b*) to encourage settlements; and
> (*c*) to provide further for the welfare of the children of the family;
> having regard to the desirability of achieving greater simplication and the saving of costs.

This Committee produced a Green Paper in 1983 to which the Board for Social Responsibility made a response early in 1984. In July 1985 the Committee published its final report. The report is a thorough and comprehensive review of divorce procedure and divorce law. This is not the time or place for an exhaustive comment on all its recommendations. However, it is worth noting that its recommendations would represent a move towards a more personal involvement of the couple in the procedure. It proposes, for example, that where children are involved or the petition is defended, there should be an initial hearing within ten weeks of the petition being lodged, attended by the couple and their legal advisers if they desire, and with access to conciliation services. To quote from their report:[1]

> The proposal for an initial hearing, at least in cases involving children, received overwhelming support from those who responded to the Consultation Paper, and we remain of the view that at an early stage in a matrimonial suit such a hearing should take place. We make our detailed recommendations in Part IV of this Report, but in outline we now propose that within about 10 weeks of the filing of divorce proceedings there should be an initial hearing, to be attended by both parties with their legal advisers if so desired, in every case involving a child to whom section 41 of the 1973 Act applies and also in cases where the respondent has stated an intention to oppose the grant of a decree. The purpose of the hearing will be to make orders in respect of agreed matters, including the decree, to refer the parties to conciliation where appropriate, to define the issues remaining between them and to give directions . . .

> The primary objective of the initial hearing will be to promote and give effect to agreements. The court will encourage the parties to reach a solution, with the help of conciliation where it is thought appropriate.

118. The Board for Social Responsibility's submission in response to the Booth Committee Green Paper supported further ideas for the reform of procedure in matrimonial and family law. In particular it came out in favour of the idea of family courts, as recommended by the Finer Committee Report (which Mr [now His Honour Judge] Quentin Edwards had argued for in *Putting Asunder*) to be staffed by people properly trained for helping with matrimonial and family matters. It is felt that such courts would offer a more humane and caring service to people in distress and show more public concern for the importance of the institution of marriage at a time when it is under pressure.

Conciliation

119. The Booth Committee Report's recommendation that adequate conciliation services should be available to the courts is in line with a growing range of opinion in favour of such developments. We must, of course, be careful to distinguish between conciliation and reconciliation.

---

[1] Paragraphs 3.5 and 3.6

Conciliation does not have as its aim the reconciliation of the parties. It aims to provide skilled help to enable the parties to agree on the arrangements to be made concerning such matters as the custody of their children and financial provision in the event of their separation or divorce. We have received some evidence from those working in this field that some couples who petition for divorce find sufficient reconciliation through the process of conciliation for them not to wish to proceed with divorce. Paragraph 4.2 of the Booth Committee's 1983 Consultative Paper said:

> There is evidence that conciliation can lead to reconciliation, sometimes in apparently unpromising cases.

Clearly, helping the parties to talk the issues out and reach agreements with the support of trained personnel is in everyone's interests. The debate about the respective value of 'in court' or 'out of court' conciliation services continues. Again, the Board for Social Responsibility expressed its support for the development of proper conciliation services.

120. It is possible that the whole atmosphere of concern about the way the present procedures seem to be undermining respect for the institution of marriage might be changed by: *(a)* the development of good family courts staffed by trained personnel and with good facilities available for couples and families seeking help, *(b)* the introduction of skilled conciliation services to the process and the use of preliminary hearings to help resolve disputes and to enable issues to be talked through in a supportive environment, and *(c)* the professional training of lawyers and others involved in the counselling of spouses whose marriage is under strain, emphasising that divorce is to be regarded as the remedy of last resort so that a petition should not be filed until all other possible solutions have been explored. If divorce is inevitable, we accept that the position will often be exacerbated by unnecessary delay; on the other hand, the evidence presented to us indicates that some spouses, whose marriages might be saved, are being pushed into divorce without giving proper thought to their acts or their consequences. We are convinced that it is essential to establish some machinery which will give parties in the latter category the opportunity to pause before they embark on proceedings which will almost inevitably lead to a decree of divorce.

The Ground and the Facts

121. The third area under review concerns the relationship between

the irretrievable breakdown of the marriage as the sole ground for divorce and the five facts necessary to establish it. The proof of any one of these facts raises a legal presumption that the marriage has irretrievably broken down, which is virtually irrefutable, at least if the petition is undefended. This means, in practice, that each of the facts is, in effect, a ground for divorce. We still await the views of the Law Commission on this matter. If the basis of the law remains unchanged and if irretrievable breakdown is still to be the sole ground for divorce, there clearly needs to be a proper procedure to determine whether a marriage has broken down beyond retrieval. The facts must be seen in practice as well as in theory, to demonstrate the truthfulness of the one ground for divorce.

122. The Church must judge whether developments in the substantive law and the procedure relating to divorce have had such a deleterious effect on the legal view of marriage that it is no longer possible to hold the opinion that this can be recognised as marriage as understood in the rites, ceremonies and the Canon law of the Church of England. We as a group have no doubt that it can be recognised as marriage by the Church. The fact that it is now easier to get out of marriage does not, in our opinion, mean that the institution has changed *per se*. To the contrary, the increase in the number of divorces every year may reflect a higher expectation of marriage held in society generally. If a particular couple's marriage fails to come up to that expectation, they are tempted to seek its dissolution and to form a new partnership in the hope that they will find in the second what they failed to find in the first. We should feel obliged to take a different view about the recognition of marriage if, for example, Parliament were to change the definition formulated in *Hyde v. Hyde* (set out in para. 100 above). But we wish to say as firmly as we can that in our view there have been no changes in the law which have fundamentally altered the basic legal character of the institution in England as a lifelong and exclusive union.

CHAPTER 4

Social Trends

123. What is happening to marriage in our society? As we have noted in Chapter 3, many people, including members of the Churches, are anxious about present trends in these matters. It is important that we get the facts right and make a dispassionate assessment of what such information is telling us. A great deal of information is available to us from research and from public surveys concerning social trends in marriage and family experience. It is important to remember that such information does not of itself answer our questions. It is evidence which requires interpretation. The Study Commission on the Family noted in 1980:

> There has undoubtedly been a shift in certain forms of behaviour and in attitudes and beliefs about some aspects of family life. What changes have taken place, and do they constitute simply adjustments to changing circumstances or a more fundamental change in values?[1]

124. A clear distinction needs to be made between actual preferences and ideals of what 'ought' to be preferred. People can hold one set of values for themselves and a completely different set for other people; whilst they can actually behave in yet another way. We may give intellectual assent to certain values, whilst our actions show we are motivated by a different set. We can act one way as individuals, whereas we may behave differently as members of groups. There is always a certain ambivalence in each of us, due to conflicting pressures and changing circumstances.

125. Some of the statistics can be interpreted, at first sight, to indicate a decline in the value placed on marriage, but these same statistics can also be interpreted to show that the institution of marriage is more popular than ever, and that those entering it do so with high ideals, even

---

[1] *Happy Families?* Study Commission on the Family, 1980. For works consulted in the preparation of this chapter see Appendix 6.

if they are less prepared to persevere with difficulty. How do we interpret the changes that have taken place? Do they constitute a departure from Christian values and teaching concerning marriage? What are the major areas of Christian concern?

POPULARITY OF MARRIAGE

126.   The proportion of the population entering into marriage has, until very recent times, risen steadily throughout this century. The number of women aged 20–39 in every thousand who were married in 1911 was 352; in 1931, 572; in 1951, 731; in 1961, 808. By the mid-1970s the proportion for women was 95 per cent and for men 91 per cent by the age of 40 (*Demographic Review 1977*, HMSO, p.54). These figures are, at least in part, affected by the availability of partners for marriage. Different mortality rates, the need to emigrate to find work, and the ravages of war all had the effect of taking away significant proportions of single men who might otherwise have sought marriage. Nevertheless, whatever else may be said, the plain fact of the popularity of the institution of marriage in modern times is demonstrated in these figures.

127.   The figures for the modern period reveal changing patterns in the marital status of those seeking marriage. Tables 1 and 2 (p.46) provide us with the historical perspective. There has been a steady increase in the number of marriages where one or both of the parties has been divorced. The growth in the rate of divorce and the impact of the availability of divorce under the new law from 1971 onwards can be detected in these figures. See Diagram 1 on p.47.

128.   Two contrasting but not necessarily contradictory comments can be made about this. The first is to note the increase in the number of people who experience second and further marriages following divorce, which raises questions about the seriousness of the life-long commitment of the partners in such marriages. The second is to note the continuing and developing popularity of marriage in spite of the traumatic experience of the breakdown of marriage leading to divorce. It may be that the image of marriage given to the young, and reinforced by the media, is more aligned to fantasy than to reality, so that the possibility of encountering difficulties is ignored or belittled and romantic expectations are raised to an unrealistic level. When these expectations are disappointed, the ethos of society leads the young to try again in their search for the perfect relationship rather than persevere in trying to find a way through the difficulties of the existing one.

NUMBER OF MARRIAGES

TABLE 1

MARRIAGES (thousands):	1901	1911	1931	1951
First marriages for both parties	253	272	307	329
First marriage for one party only	28	25	28	51
Second (or later) marriage for both parties:				
both divorced }	10	9	10	22
one or both widowed }				
Total	291	307	344	402
Remarriage* as percentage of all marriages	13.1	11.4	11.0	18.1
First Marriages				
Average age of marrying (years)				
Bachelors	27.2	27.3	27.4	26.8
Spinsters	25.6	25.6	25.5	24.6
Remarriages				
Average age of remarrying (years)				
Men widowed or divorced	45.5	46.2	49.2	46.5
Women widowed or divorced	40.6	41.5	44.3	40.9

Sources: *Social Trends 8*, table 2.10; *Social Trends 9*, table 2.11; *Social Trends 11*, table 2.9.
* for one or both parties.

TABLE 2

MARRIAGES (thousands)	1961	1971	1976	1981	1983	1984	1985	1986
First marriage for both partners	340	369	282	263	255	259	257	254
First marriage for one partner only								
Bachelor/divorced woman	11	21	30	32	32	32	32	34
Bachelor/widow	5	4	4	3	2	2	2	2
Spinster/divorced man	12	24	32	36	37	38	38	38
Spinster/widower	8	5	4	3	2	2	2	2
Second (or later) marriage for both partners								
Both divorced	5	17	34	44	45	46	47	48
Both widowed	10	10	10	7	7	6	6	6
Divorced man/widow	3	4	5	5	4	5	4	4
Divorced woman/widower	3	5	5	5	5	5	5	5
Total marriages	397	459	406	398	389	396	393	394
Remarriages* as a percentage of all marriages	14	20	31	34	35	35	35	35
Remarriages* of the divorced as a percentage of all marriages	9	15	26	31	32	32	32	33

* Remarriage for one or both partners.   Source: *Social Trends 17*, table 2.12 (1961–1986).

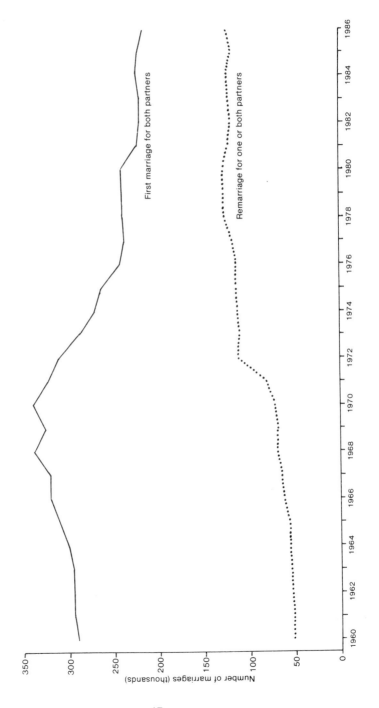

DIAGRAM 1 NUMBER OF FIRST MARRIAGES AND REMARRIAGES, 1960–84, ENGLAND AND WALES

First marriage for both partners

Remarriage for one or both partners

Number of marriages (thousands)

THE AGE AT WHICH PEOPLE MARRY

129. The trend towards earlier marriage, which can be evidenced from the mid-nineteenth century onwards, has been reversed in very recent years. Those born in 1850 married at an average age of 27 (men) and 26 (women). The proportion of teenage brides steadily rose throughout the twentieth century. In 1971, 10 per cent of bachelors marrying were under 20 and 31 per cent of spinsters. The proportions have been particularly high for spinsters in social classes IV and V. During the 1970s the number of spinsters marrying in their teens almost halved and this has continued to decline by at least 9 per cent per annum for every year since 1980. Approximately 5 per cent of bachelors were under 20 and 18 per cent of spinsters at the time of their marriage in 1984. This trend has continued in 1985. According to *Social Trends 17*, the reduction in the number of teenage spinsters marrying has never been less than 9 per cent for each year since 1980.

130. The reasons for this are many and may include less pressure on pregnant teenagers to get married, easier abortion (32 per cent of teenage conceptions ended in abortion in 1982 compared with 21 per cent in 1972), and increase in the practice of cohabitation and the changing cultural and social experience of women in our society.

131. It is possible that the effect of this rise in the average age of marriages involving bachelors and spinsters will be to help steady the figures for divorce, since past experience seems to demonstrate that there is a clear link between the age at which people marry and their vulnerability to marriage breakdown and divorce. On the whole it would seem that the younger people marry the more prone they are to divorce in later years. We may well experience some decline in divorce levels among those marrying for the first time.

WHERE PEOPLE MARRY

132. People contract their marriages in one of three ways: by civil ceremony, the Church of England's ceremony, or by other religious ceremonies. The figures for the manner of solemnisation since 1971 are as follows:

TABLE 3 MANNER OF SOLEMNISATION (ENGLAND AND WALES)

	1971	1976	1980	1981	1982	1983	1984	1985	1986
Civil Ceremonies	187,101	179,330	183,395	172,514	185,080	187,327	170,506	169,025	168,255
First marriage for both	97,561	82,390	76,469	71,530	67,788	67,688	69,554	70,124	67,981
Remarriage for one or both	69,540	96,940	106,926	100,984	97,301	99,639	100,952	98,901	100,274
Religious Ceremonies	237,636	179,237	186,627	179,459	177,077	177,007	178,680	177,364	179,669
First marriage for both	222,786	161,380	164,532	156,183	152,639	153,261	154,461	151,803	152,391
Remarriage for one or both	14,850	17,857	22,095	23,276	24,438	23,746	24,219	25,561	27,278
Church of England*	160,165	119,569	123,400	118,435	116,978	116,854	117,506	116,378	117,804
Other religious ceremonies	77,471	59,668	63,227	61,024	60,099	60,153	61,174	60,986	61,865

* including the Church in Wales.

133. It would seem that in the period 1971–1976 there was a steady decline in the proportion both of weddings conducted in Anglican churches and in all religious weddings. Since 1976 the figures have slightly recovered and steadied so that approximately 33 per cent of couples marry by Anglican rites and a further 18 per cent by other religious ceremonies. Thus it would seem that approximately one-third of all couples exercise their right to be married in the Church of England. The 1981 census figures demonstrate considerable regional variation. 62 per cent of marriages in Greater London in 1981 were contracted by civil ceremony and 38 per cent by religious ceremony. In the West Midlands the figure was 50 per cent for each. In Cheshire 59 per cent of marriages were by religious ceremony and 41 per cent by civil ceremony. In Merseyside, which has a strong Roman Catholic presence, 57 per cent were by religious ceremony and 43 per cent by civil ceremony. A variety of influences may account for regional variation

An Honourable Estate

and these are likely to include the size of population of different religious groups, the social class composition of an area, and the presence of sizeable populations of other faiths. It is probable that there is a corresponding variation by social class, with social classes IV and V less likely to seek marriage in the Church of England. The figures are likely to vary again for the different ethnic communities, where there are significant proportions of people who belong either to Christian Churches other than the Church of England or to other faiths than the Christian religion.

COHABITATION

134.   There has been a growing trend for couples to live together on a regular basis outside marriage. The very high proportion of people entering marriage (see para. 126) encourages the view that cohabitation is still predominantly a prelude to marriage rather than an alternative to it. From 1966–70, 3 per cent of couples married for the first time gave a common address before their marriage. In the period 1971–75 the figure had grown to 10 per cent. The figure has continued to grow to over 20 per cent of couples entering marriage. Table 4 illustrates the growth of cohabitation when seen as a proportion of women aged 18–49. In 1979 2.7 per cent of women aged 18–49 were cohabiting. By 1984 this figure had risen to 4.2 per cent–a sharp rise in a relatively short period.

TABLE 4   GROWTH IN COHABITATION BY WOMEN

Great Britain   *Percentage and numbers*

	1979	1981	1982	1983	1984
Age group (percentages)					
18–24	4.5	5.6	6.1	5.2	7.3
25–49	2.2	2.6	3.2	3.2	3.3
All aged 18–49	2.7	3.3	3.8	3.6	4.2
Women in sample (=100%) (numbers)					
18–24	1,353	1,517	1,250	1,191	1,174
25–49	4,651	5,007	4,246	4,094	4,070
All aged 18–49	6,004	6,524	5,496	5,285	5,244

Source: *Social Trends 17*, table 2.11.
       No later information is yet available (September 1987).

50

135. The growth in the illegitimacy rates and in the proportion of these births registered in the name of both parents indicates that cohabitation often extends beyond the birth of a child. In 1961, 48,000 out of 811,000 (approx.) live births were illegitimate (6 per cent). In 1984 this had risen to 110,000 out of 637,000 live births (17 per cent). Of these, 38 per cent were registered by both parents in 1961 and 63 per cent in 1984. (See Table 5.)

TABLE 5 ILLEGITIMACY

	Illegitimate live births (thousands)	*As percentage of total live births*	*Percentage registered in joint names*
England and Wales			
1961	48	6	38
1971	66	8	45
1976	54	9	51
1981	81	13	58
1984	110	17	63
1985	126	19	65
1986	141	21	66
United Kingdom			
1985	142	19	—
1986	158	21	—

Source: *Social Trends 17*, 2:20.

136. Cohabitation challenges the Christian understanding of fidelity and monogamy in the marital relationship. Though many young cohabiting couples would deny any charge of promiscuity or even of infidelity, what cannot be in doubt is the partial nature of the commitment they appear to be prepared to make to each other. Recent surveys[1] carried out indicate that 78 per cent of people in the UK believed that they should not commit adultery, and this was a much higher proportion than in any other European country. However, it also has to be said that the same sample believed that only 25 per cent of other people lived up to that standard. This could indicate that whilst fidelity and monogamy are still valued, they are not valued as highly as other qualities such as understanding and companionship.

---

[1] *Values and Social Change in Britain*, Ed. M. Abrams, G. Gerard and N. Timms, pub. Macmillan, p.61

137. For a significant minority, marriage no longer represents the point at which the couple start to live together on a regular basis. Moreover, some of these do not formalise their relationship when establishing a family, even though the offspring are thus illegitimate. It is possible that this means that future patterns will include a significant proportion of couples for whom cohabitation is a permanent alternative to marriage rather than a preliminary to it. Nevertheless, for a very large majority of couples marriage represents the point at which they live together on a regular and permanent basis.

DIVORCE

138. The figures (in thousands) for divorce in England and Wales are as follows:

	1951	1961	1966	1971	1976	1980	1981	1983	1984	1985	1986
Petitions filed	38	32	47	111	145	172	170	169	180	191	180
Decrees nisi granted	30	27	41	89	132	151	148	150	148	162	153
Decrees absolute	29	25	39	74	127	148	146	147	145	160	153

Source: *Social Trends 17*, table 2.15.

Taking into account the effect on the figures of the accelerated rise after the war and the immediate impact of the operation of the new legislation in 1971, there is a steady rise over the whole period. The percentage rise was continuous until the mid-1970s. Since then it has steadied at an annual rate of approximately 12 per 1,000 of married couples in England and Wales (it had been 2 in 1961). The 1985 figures represent the first year to reflect the impact of the 1984 Matrimonial and Family Proceedings Act. See Diagram 2 on p.53.

139. The proportion of divorces involving at least one partner who was divorced immediately before their most recent marriage has increased from 9 per cent in 1971, to 21 per cent in 1984. Of all divorces in 1971, 89 per cent were to couples who had married as bachelors and spinsters, whereas the proportion had fallen to 78 per cent of all couples who divorced in 1984. (It should be borne in mind, of course, that over the period concerned the proportion of all married couples at risk of divorcing who had married as bachelors and spinsters had also declined – a growing proportion of all marriages – during the 1970s especially – having involved at least one divorced partner.) Marriages contracted by those under 20 are twice as likely to end in divorce as those contracted

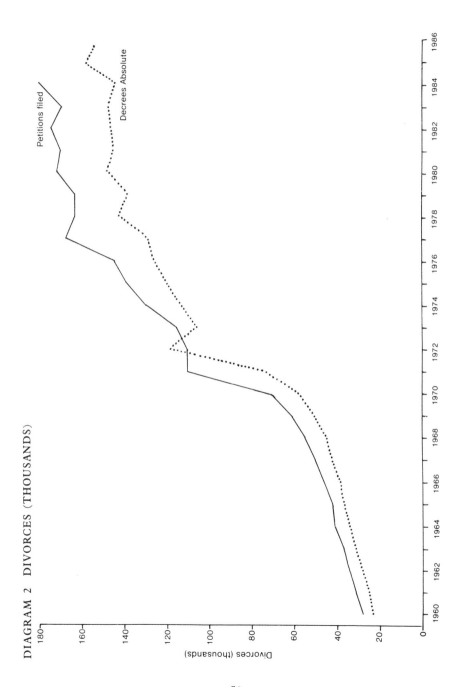

DIAGRAM 2 DIVORCES (THOUSANDS)

Petitions filed

Decrees Absolute

Divorces (thousands)

180
160
140
120
100
80
60
40
20
0

1960 1962 1964 1966 1968 1970 1972 1974 1976 1978 1980 1982 1984 1986

by those over 20.[1] Since there has been a noticeable drop in the proportion of all marriages in which brides and bridegrooms marry as teenagers, this may partially explain the steadying of the rate of divorce and its decline among those marrying for the first time. On the other hand, the growing proportion of couples where one or both partners have previously been divorced might be expected to have acted to increase the overall divorce rate. The number of petitions showed a sharp increase in 1985 but in 1986 fell back to virtually the same level as 1984. This is no doubt explained by the fact that 1985 was the first full year of operation of section 1 of the 1984 Act, mentioned in para. 114, which allows a petition for divorce after one year of marriage. (Previously, for the first three years a petitioner had to prove exceptional hardship to them or exceptional depravity on the part of the respondent in order to obtain leave to present a petition.) The figure for 1985 therefore includes petitions which would otherwise not have been presented until 1986 or 1987.

140.   In over 70 per cent of the divorces granted in 1985 the woman was the petitioner. Where the man was the petitioner the most frequent fact alleged in the case was adultery, followed by separation for two years with consent. 'Unreasonable behaviour' only accounted for approximately 16 per cent of cases in which the husband was the petitioner. In cases where the wife was the petitioner the most common fact alleged was 'unreasonable behaviour' which accounted for almost one-half of such petitions – nearly double the proportion for adultery and more than double for separation for two years with consent (see Diagram 3, p.55).

141.   The percentage of divorces involving children under sixteen has varied little since 1971 when it represented 57 per cent of the total. It rose to 60 per cent by 1978 but has since fallen back to 57 per cent in 1984. There has been a steady increase throughout the period since 1951 in the percentage of all divorces involving couples in the first four years of marriage. In 1951 this represented 10 per cent of the total; in 1971, 13 per cent; in 1976, 18 per cent; in 1979, 19 per cent; and in 1984, 22 per cent. The median duration of marriages ending in divorce is just over 10 years.

---

[1] Detailed figures are set out in *Marriage and Divorce Statistics*, 1981, Office of Population Censuses and Surveys, cf. Tables 3.3 and 4.2. See also: *Marital status before marriage and age at marriage: their influence on the chance of divorce*, John Haskey, Population Trends 32.

DIAGRAM 3 DIVORCE–PARTY GRANTED DECREE: BY GROUNDS

England and Wales

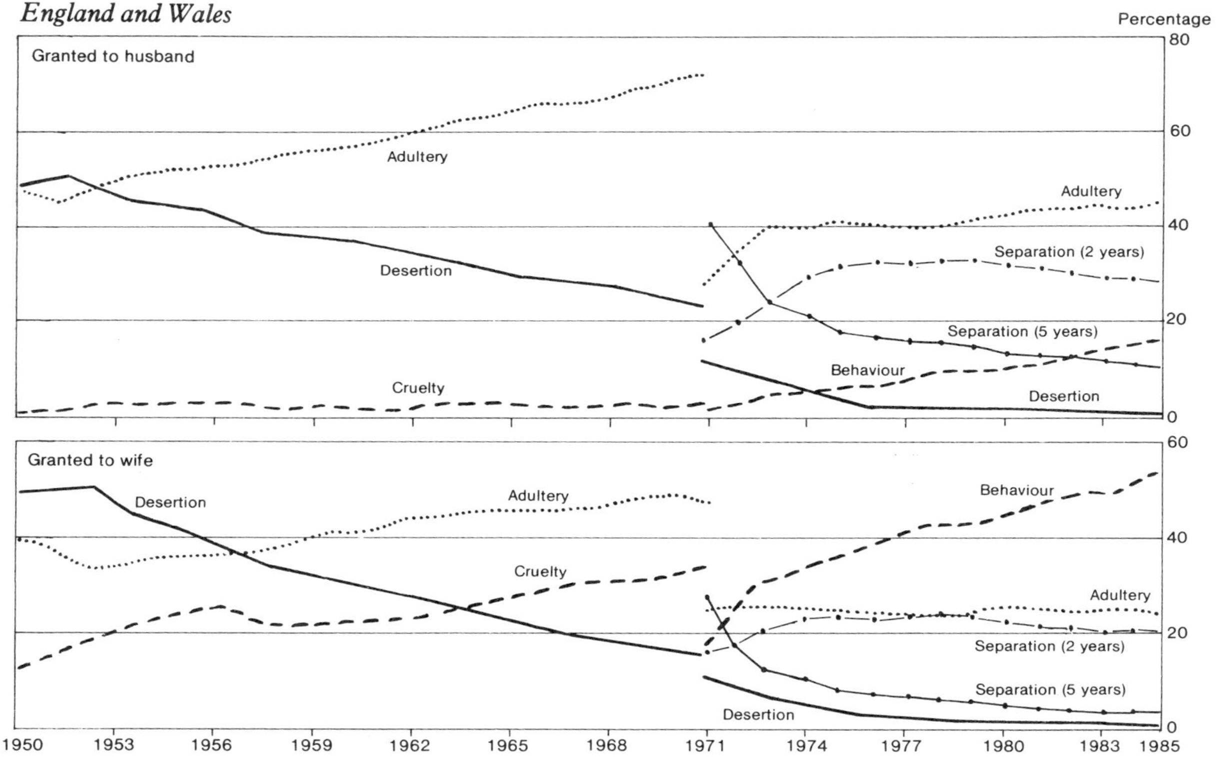
Percentage
Granted to husband
Adultery
Desertion
Cruelty
Adultery
Separation (2 years)
Separation (5 years)
Behaviour
Desertion
Granted to wife
Desertion
Adultery
Cruelty
Behaviour
Adultery
Separation (2 years)
Separation (5 years)
Desertion
80
60
40
20
0
60
40
20
0
1950
1953
1956
1959
1962
1965
1968
1971
1974
1977
1980
1983
1985

[1] Decrees granted to one party on more than one ground are included in the 100 per cent base but have not been plotted.
[2] The Divorce Reform Act 1969 came into effect in 1971.

Source: Office of Population Censuses and Surveys, *Social Trends 17*.

142. Two conclusions may reasonably be drawn from these figures. First, marriages contracted by persons under the age of 20 are much more vulnerable to divorce (see para. 136). This may be to do with the maturity of the persons involved and/or the circumstances surrounding the marriage (e.g. parental and social pressure in the event of a pregnancy). It is not to suggest that many marriages contracted in this period are not highly successful. Second, there would appear to be no truth in the idea that second and subsequent marriages are more likely to succeed than first marriages. On the 1980/81 figures the chance that the marriage of a divorced man would again end in divorce is 1.5 times that of a single man who marries at the same age. First marriages are more durable than second and subsequent marriages.

143. Institutions are never fully in line with the relational needs which they are meant to serve. The growth in cohabitation, for example, suggests that the form of marriage in our society is not matching the felt needs of some couples. The same is true for divorce. The level of marriage breakdown cannot be absolutely equated with the rate of divorce. Some couples simply separate, others obtain a separation order from the Courts. Some couples who continue to maintain the legal reality of their marriage may well have experienced a breakdown of the relationship within their marriage.

REMARRIAGE

144. The experience of divorce does not seem to have led to any significant drift away from marriage. Instead it has led to an increase in the proportion of marriages which are second or subsequent marriages for one or both of the parties. In 9 per cent of the total number of marriages in 1961 one or both of the parties had been divorced. In 1971 the figure had risen to 20 per cent; in 1976, 26 per cent; in 1981, 31 per cent; and in 1985 to 32 per cent. (This figure has remained stable in the last few years. Table 6 gives a breakdown of where people were married and indicates the number of marriages conducted by religious ceremony where one or both of the parties have been divorced.) Thus a third of all marriages involve at least one partner who has been divorced. We need to bear in mind that this increase is due to the increasing number of people available for remarriage, rather than to any increased trend among divorced people to remarry.

FAMILIES

145. The diagram produced by the Family Policy Studies Centre on

TABLE 6 MANNER OF SOLEMNISATION OF MARRIAGES   COMBINATIONS OF PREVIOUS MARITAL CONDITION, England and Wales   1981

Marital status	All marriages	With civil ceremonies	With religious ceremonies								
			Church of England and Church in Wales	Roman Catholics	Other denominations excluding Jews						Jews
					Methodists	Congregationalists	Baptists	United Reformed Church	Others		
All	351,973	172,514	118,435	26,097	16,832	1,065	4,053	6,627	5,309	1,041
Bachelor marrying:										
Spinster	227,713	71,530	114,143	24,447	7,528	681	2,469	2,386	3,676	853
Widow	2,315	1,382	599	176	75	5	14	20	41	3
Divorced woman	29,078	24,326	314	365	2,194	91	357	1,024	365	42
Widower marrying:										
Spinster	2,446	1,339	680	154	104	6	50	39	69	5
Widow	6,605	3,793	1,727	329	368	19	106	112	110	41
Divorced woman	4,717	4,035	67	43	297	12	51	137	67	8
Divorced man marrying:										
Spinster	33,209	24,581	639	494	4,189	157	642	1,890	579	38
Widow	4,538	3,904	45	28	290	12	62	126	61	10
Divorced woman	41,352	37,624	221	61	1,787	82	302	893	341	41

(Marriage and Divorce Statistics, 1981, Office of Population Censuses and Surveys.)

Families by type sets out the present picture. The figures are for 1980–82.

DIAGRAM 4 FAMILIES BY TYPE

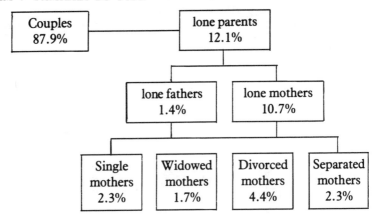

146.   These facts concerning marriage and divorce have had an impact on family life. Marriage leads on into family experience. Approximately 9 out of 10 women will have children at some stage in their lives. By 1985 the percentage of households with dependent children headed by a lone parent had risen to 14 per cent, of which 12 per cent were lone mother households. In spite of this worrying trend we should note that approximately 84 per cent of all children at that date were living with both their natural parents. However, the figure for lone parent families is projected to continue to rise. In 1981 there were approximately 1.4 million one parent households. By 2001 this figure is projected to rise to 1.8 million.

147.   It is not possible, in this Report, to enter into a detailed debate on all the changes in the past few decades which have affected people's attitudes to marriage and family life. There has been a range of developments in our culture which have had a profound effect upon the way people experience marriage and family. There is the impact, for example, of the development of safe contraceptive protection which has both allowed couples the opportunity to plan their families and contributed to the steady reduction in the size of families in Britain in the twentieth century. Along with the changes brought about by the widespread use of safe contraceptive devices has been the changing attitude towards sexual matters. There is a much greater openness about these issues, especially among younger people. The availability of contraception in the context of changing public attitudes has opened the

way for a greater stress on the enjoyment of sexual relations for their own sake. There have been major changes in the place and role of women in our society which have increased the opportunities for women to exercise greater independence. For example, a greater proportion of married women are in paid employment in our society and are not, thereby, as financially dependent on their partners as in the past. Greater longevity is another factor which marks our age from past ages. Neither marriage nor families are as prone as once they were to the intrusion of death at a relatively early age. Marriages are therefore much more likely *(a)* to be made up of couples both of whom have independent contributions to make to society, *(b)* to last longer, when terminated by death rather than by divorce, *(c)* to lead to smaller families, demanding a shorter time-span for full-time child rearing, and *(d)* in general, to be open to a greater degree of choice than was often the case in previous ages.

148.   Other areas of public policy which relate to and affect marriages include such specific matters as taxation and housing policies. In recent years there has been strong pressure to reform the way married couples are assessed for purposes of income tax. The present system, which involves the wife's income (or in the case of separate assessment, unearned income) having to be declared by the husband who is then liable for the tax, is manifestly unjust and out of date. There are still a number of important aspects of the law relating to married couples concerning finances which view the wife in terms of her husband. These concerns extend to such matters as mortgage tax relief. Married couples may claim relief on the interest on a £30,000 mortgage. Couples living together outside marriage can claim the relief on £60,000 where the house is owned jointly. These should not be viewed simply as technical matters, since they illustrate the difficulty of keeping public policy in step with the needs of people who are able to sustain and uphold the institution of marriage in a changing society. There can be little doubt that these and other factors have had a profound impact on the perceived understandings and expectations of marriage in our society.

149.   So far as Parliament is concerned, value issues about the family have often been the most controversial, and have been those on which the political parties have been most unwilling to take a stand. Legislation on divorce and abortion has been the result of private members' action taken on a free vote in the House of Commons. Such debates have followed years of heated national discussion, and even when a decision has been taken it can result in further anomalies.

150.   In a period of rapid social and economic change, many people will be faced with uncertainty and a consequent sense of insecurity. Change always involves costs to be paid, as well as benefits to be gained. Change has also increased diversity and the availability of choice, which has a considerable impact on traditional values. But pluralism, denoting as it does a wide range of individual beliefs, does not necessarily mean that variety cannot be accommodated within a consensus of agreed basic values.

151.   Marriage is not about to disappear. We live in an age where marriage is popular and where there are high expectations of it; marriages are also expected to last much longer than in previous ages. The essential Christian value of marriage, as a lasting union between a man and a woman where children may be brought up in a healthy and secure environment, is not being seriously challenged.

152.   All this serves to demonstrate the distinctive pressures and opportunities which a couple entering marriage today can reasonably expect to face. The complex social changes which have taken place around marriage and the family provide part of the background to the concerns which are at the heart of this Report.

CHAPTER 5

The Options

153. The Working Party has given careful consideration to the main choices for public policy which the Church might ask for on this question. Evidence has been submitted to us in support of each of the choices. There are, we believe, five broad options. We turn now to examine these and to set out our own responses to each one. The options are:

   I The introduction of universal civil marriage, leaving the civil authority with the sole responsibility for the conduct of all marriages.

   II To remove the obligation of the Church of England to conduct marriages and thus to place it on the same footing in these matters as the other Churches.

   III To restrict marriage in the Church of England to couples where at least one of the parties is baptised.

   IV To introduce universal civil preliminaries, leaving the Church with its obligation in the actual conduct of the marriage ceremony.

   V To affirm the present position and to continue to make full use of the opportunities it offers to the Church.

The Working Party is unanimous in recommending this fifth option. It should be noted that we did not start out sharing the same view. Our unanimity has been arrived at in the process of our work as a group. Part of the reason for this has been our response to the alternative possibilities. We have given these very full consideration and believe it right to start by examining them and setting out our response to them before returning to our own chosen option.

OPTION I

The Introduction of Universal Civil Marriage

154. This option gives to the civil authority the sole responsibility for conducting all marriages. Everyone would be required to go through a civil ceremony in order to be married according to the law (the so-called 'continental' system, described in paras 77 onwards). That would mean that in England every couple would be required to be married at the

61

Register Office where they would take each other as man and wife in the presence of the Superintendent Registrar and Registrar and witnesses. It would no longer be possible to be married at a religious service held in a place of worship. This proposal would not just bring to an end the obligation on the clergy of the Church of England to conduct marriages in their churches: it would end the conduct of marriages in churches and other places of worship. In effect it would introduce the Napoleonic system into England.

155. This would not preclude the possibility of religious ceremonies in addition to the civil procedure. People would be free to choose whatever further ceremonies were felt to be appropriate. These, however, would not be recognised by the law as an accepted alternative to the civil procedure.

156. In such circumstances it would be for the Churches, including the Church of England, to decide what services they wished to make available to couples at the time of their wedding and to whom they should be offered. Such religious ceremonies might take place before the civil ceremony, as was suggested by one parish priest who gave evidence to us. In countries where there now is universal civil marriage this is not allowed; those who wish to have an additional church service in such nations always have it after the civil procedure has been completed.

157. If there were to be such a change, the Church of England would need to be clear whether it would offer couples an additional marriage service or a service of blessing on a marriage which had already taken place. If the decision was to offer an additional service of marriage, it would have to be clear when the couple would be accepted as married in the eyes of the Church; or, if a 'blessing' were offered, what would be meant by that. There would be no doubt that in the eyes of the law the couple would be married in the register office. The Church would have to accept that legal position.

158. In those nations which have a system of universal civil marriage, Roman Catholic Canon law requires an additional full service of marriage in church for its members. Members are only recognised as being properly married according to the law of the Church when they have participated in the marriage service provided by the Church. Protestant Churches in countries where there is universal civil marriage have a more varied response. Some provide an additional service in

church which is seen to be a service of marriage, and Christian couples might not understand themselves to be properly married until they had participated in the Church's service of marriage. Others see their role as offering prayers, a blessing, and pastoral support to couples following their marriage by civil process.

159.   There are forceful arguments advanced in favour of such a far-reaching change. There are some who believe that the changes that have taken place in marriage in our society in recent years mean that there is now a clear difference between the understanding of marriage as held by Christians and that embodied in law and custom in our society. Some doubt whether what is now offered in Register Offices is any longer truly lifelong marriage. The suggestion is thus made that there are two kinds of marriage in our country: a Christian kind upheld by the Church, and an increasingly secular kind, based on pragmatic considerations. Those who hold this view, that there are two kinds of marriage, would see the introduction of universal civil marriage as an honest way of giving formal recognition to this fact. The Church, no longer being obliged to conduct marriages, would not be required to extend recognition to the secular view of marriage, and would be free to stress its distinctive understanding, through its own disciplines, rites and ceremonies. For those who believe that there is such a thing as Christian marriage which may only be enjoyed as a result of the sacramental ministry of the Church, or who see this as a benefit available only to Christian people, universal civil marriage would open the way for the Church to make a clear statement of its view.

160.   In response to the proposals for universal civil marriage we wish to stress that we share many of the anxieties felt by those attracted to this option. It is by no means so evident as it used to be that marriage is, in English law, a lifelong union. We cannot pretend that our exacting Christian understanding of the 'one-flesh' bond is as widely shared among our contemporaries as we could wish. Many see marriage as easily terminable; some see it as unnecessary. To shut our eyes to these trends might be, in effect, to go along with them.

161.   Nevertheless, we do not believe that the introduction of universal civil marriage is the right response to make to these serious and worrying trends. We must note that such an option is not a matter for the Church of England alone. The other Christian Churches and other religious groups in our country who are recognised for the purpose of marriage, would be affected. Since such a change would involve an

amendment to the Marriage Act 1949 the Church of England ought not to ask for it without seeking the opinion of other Churches in England and Wales. The evidence we have received indicates that they would not necessarily welcome this change. We must also note that for the Church of England to propose universal civil marriage would represent the first occasion when the introduction of universal civil marriage had been sought at the request of a Church. In other countries the introduction of universal civil marriage has always been on the initiative of the legislating authority. Churches have adapted themselves and their ministry in the light of such changes; they have never initiated them.

162. Our main reasons for not recommending this option flow from our convictions about marriage and about the duties and opportunities afforded to the Church, set out in Chapter 1. We reaffirm the view of marriage as held in successive major reports made to the Church of England over the past two decades. In particular, God's provision of marriage is for Christian and non-Christian alike. We may not, therefore, make a fundamental distinction between marriage as entered into by the rites of the Church and that which is experienced outside the Church. We believe the Root Commission made a clear statement of the Christian view:

> Christians experience marriage 'in the Lord' and its true nature and meaning are for them expressed in Christian terms; but this is not to deny in any way the reality of marriage among those outside the Christian Church. Matrimony, in the words of the Prayer Book, is 'to be honourable among all men'. Testimony must be given to the plain fact that Christian insights and the experienced reality of being 'in Christ' have transformed the lives of married Christians. But, on the other hand, there is no such entity as 'Christian marriage', except in the sense of the marriage of Christian men and women. God is generous in bestowing grace, and he does not confine his gifts within the Christian dispensation, and so what matrimony is may sometimes be as clearly seen in a non-Christian marriage as in a Christian one. (para. 24)

We agree with this. We do not believe it would be right, in current circumstances, for the Church to draw such a clear line between civil practice and Church practice.

163. We are, none the less, concerned at many of the trends in our society, though it is important to come to the right conclusions in the face of such evidence. That there are many in our society who have an inadequate understanding of marriage and a weak commitment to making it succeed, should not necessarily lead us to conclude that the

formal understanding of marriage in law is inadequate and weak. There is an important task to be done in strengthening people's understanding of and commitment to marriage. For all the serious pressure on it, there has been no significant change in the conditions pertaining to marriage in the law of our country. A marriage may only be contracted in this country between one man and one woman who are of an age to marry, who freely and publicly give their consent and who are not in law married to anyone else. Such marriages may only be terminated by death or divorce. No other relationships may, in law, be recognised as marriage. We believe that, irrespective of whether couples enter marriage in the context of a religious ceremony or by a civil ceremony, the commitment which they have undertaken is still marriage as understood in the Christian tradition (see Chapter 3). Moving to universal civil marriage would undermine that basic conviction and would promote the notion of two understandings of marriage. Such a proposition has all the characteristics of a self-fulfilling prophecy.

164.   We believe the Church should view its responsibilities in the field of marriage as an opportunity. In a society in which about half of all the couples who get married each year do so in the context of a Christian ceremony, it is surprising that there should be suggestions recommending universal civil marriage. The Churches have here an unrivalled opportunity to influence for good the public understanding of marriage and public policies on marriage. The Church of England has a particular responsibility in this area; one-third of all English marriages take place in the Church of England. That so many couples seek our help at the moment of their marriage, and this in the setting of a multi-cultural and pluralist society, is a high responsibility and a major opportunity to offer care to all who seek to avail themselves of it. We believe that the Church should continue to make full use of such opportunities and give thought to the way they might be used to help strengthen the understanding and experience of marriage in society. In our view, it would be disastrous for the Church even to appear to wish to distance itself from ministering to any and all who might seek its ministry at such a crucial moment in their personal development and relationships. The evidence of the Mothers' Union survey (Appendix 2) would seem to indicate that our view of this option is widely held in the Church.

OPTION II

To Place the Church of England on the same Footing in Law
with Regard to Marriage as other Churches

165.   The effect of this would be to take away the rights which all

parishioners (except divorced people whose previous partner is still living) have in law to be able to have their marriages contracted by Church of England rites.[1] Couples would only be entitled to be married in the Church of England if the Church was willing to act. There would be no obligation. The Church would have to develop its own laws and customs for deciding who was and who was not entitled to be married in church.

166. The arguments presented to us in favour of this option are based on social, pastoral and theological considerations, although these cannot be neatly distinguished. Critics are suggesting that it is no longer appropriate for the Church of England to possess such privileges in a society which includes significant groups of citizens of other faiths or of none. Two-thirds of all couples choose to be married in places other than the Church of England, and we welcome this availability of choice. At its lowest, the Church of England provides an alternative method to the register office of contracting a marriage. On the Church's side there is indeed the privilege and responsibility of ministering not only to its own members, but also to many whose contact with the Church has been small; viewed from the other side, the privilege is that of the parishioner. It is this 'privilege', of course, which gives rise to the pastoral and theological issues which trouble some people.

167. We acknowledge that there is pressure on some clergy, particularly with large parishes or well-placed churches, to officiate at many weddings, and we recognise the real dilemma this poses simply through weight of numbers. There is, however, a more substantial issue. We accept that clergy are sometimes, and indeed often, asked to conduct services of marriage for couples who show no sign of having any commitment to the Christian faith at all, for it is indeed possible in law for non-believers, or even members of other faiths (though we know of no actual instances of that), to have their marriages conducted in the Church of England.

168. It has been suggested to us that in the present age, when many approach marriage with little understanding of what it means in Christian teaching, the clergy would be helped to challenge couples towards a deeper understanding if they had a discretion to decline to conduct the service. Any clergyman asked to officiate at a marriage will,

[1] See Chapter 3, para. 94, and Appendix 1.

of course, wish to bring the couple to a sensitive and profound Christian understanding of what they are about. We do not believe that the power to reject any couple would do anything to achieve that aim. Rejection it would be, for surely no priest would say no until he had seen them. The knowledge that they could say no would itself place a difficult burden on clergy in differentiating between couples; anomalous situations would occur in neighbouring parishes. Recent attempts to agree criteria for the marriage of a couple, one or both of whom are divorced with the former spouse still alive, do not give grounds for confidence that there could be agreed criteria on which to make such a selection.

169.　In our view it is better that the right or 'privilege' to have a marriage celebrated in the parish church is widely known. We appreciate the anxiety of some, but at least it enables the clergyman to impress on the couple a Christian understanding of what marriage entails, and to pray for them in their life together. For some it may be the beginning of a much more worthwhile and committed relationship. That is, in our view, the real pastoral concern–to be of service to those who may respond, and whose lives may be changed and enriched as a result.

170.　We must, however, respond to the underlying theological issues which have been raised with us. It has been said, If we marry 'all comers', what understanding of the Church is thereby demonstrated? Would not the Church be seen only as an arm of the civil authority, providing religious decoration on demand? Is not the Church a body with its own teaching, and with a recognisable membership sharing doctrine and discipline? Why should it minister to those who do not share that life and teaching? May not the whole witness of the Church be compromised, because it is shown not to take its own formularies or discipline seriously?

171.　We do not discount these arguments, which spring from a profound concern to safeguard what the Church stands for. We share the concern of those who desire to give every encouragement to clergy, and others, who seek to put forward a Christian view of marriage, and to do nothing to undermine the whole work and mission of the Church. None the less we believe this view leads inexorably to the position that the Church will, and should, serve only those already within its fold. It will withdraw from involvement in the lives of many (whose attachment to its mission and beliefs may, indeed, be minimal) at a crucial and sensitive time, when they are ready to seek its ministrations, for whatever reason and to whatever extent. At present the Church has a real opportunity to bring the seriousness of Christian teaching on marriage before them.

172.   Further, we believe that the argument fails to reckon with our conviction that marriage is not simply for believers. It is part of God's good and gracious provision for all people. If we take that view, is it a sufficient reason to decline to be involved, where our involvement is sought, because the couple have not made any Christian commitment? We believe not. At a time when a couple would have the opportunity to see how the Christian faith bears upon their marriage, we do not believe it right to take any step which would diminish that opportunity. We see in the argument too great a desire for safety, and not enough readiness to risk being instruments of grace. We could accept it if we believed that God is only active in the marriage of Christians and not others, but that is not our view. The Church's involvement in any marriage proclaims (as we believe) that God cannot be shut out of any life.

173.   Therefore we do not think that this option offers a solution to the problem and we note that this is not just an issue concerning marriage. Similar questions are raised by the duties of the Church of England with regard to baptism and to funerals. Our remit is restricted to the question of marriage. If, however, the Church were to proceed with this option it would only be able to do so after considering the question as it concerns those other occasional offices. Since these matters are part of the obligations which the Church of England has as a result of its particular historic place in our society we have to recognise that the raising of this question by the Church might well lead to Parliament considering other aspects of the legal position of the Church of England. This is not to suggest that, if this solution is right, it ought not to be pursued because of these wider matters; it is to ensure that such a solution would be adopted only in full knowledge that it is likely to raise wider questions concerning the legal position of the Church of England in this country. Similar consequences would ensue in the case of the previously discussed option of universal civil marriage.

174.   Our arguments for rejecting this proposal are not based merely on these wider complications and complexities. We do not believe that the pressures on clergy would be significantly relieved by such a change. The desire of a significant proportion of the population to have their marriages conducted within the Church of England is as much rooted in custom as it is in any understanding of rights and responsibilities. We would still have to face the pastoral challenge of couples seeking our

help at the moment of their marriage, and the problem will not be solved by giving the Church of England discretion. The evidence we have taken from other Churches in England suggests that they face similar pastoral challenges even though they do not have the same legal obligation to couples as the Church of England. As we have already said in para. 161, we believe that it would be disastrous for the Church even to appear to be shutting the door on those who seek its ministry at crucial moments in their personal development and relationships. Such moments are occasions for welcome and the present position encourages the Church to offer it generously. (See the evidence of the Mothers' Union survey in Appendix 2.) The Church of England has a responsibility to all parishioners and we believe this provides the basis for offering care to all those who seek to avail themselves of it.

175.   We recognise that couples sometimes experience pressure to choose a church wedding. These pressures do not necessarily arise from the legal position of the Church of England but from family and social expectations. Altering the legal position of the Church of England would not take away such pressures. They can only be dealt with in the context of sensitive pastoral care in the preparation for marriage. Wherever couples have their marriages conducted, they should feel welcomed and supported.

176.   Furthermore, in the evidence offered to us from other Churches in England, we have not been encouraged to seek for this change. There is no pressure from our ecumenical partners for the Church of England to seek to have its position changed in this way.

OPTION III

To Restrict Marriage in the Church of England to Couples
where at least one of the Parties is Baptised

177.   The legal position on this matter is considered in some detail in Appendix 1 (pp.78–84). We set out in that Appendix how the common law right to marry in church was dealt with in the Chadwick Commission Report of 1970, *Church and State*, and follow this with comments from the Legal Adviser to the General Synod, and relevant opinions from text books of Ecclesiastical and Canon Law. Brief reference is made in the Appendix (para. 14) to the acceptance by the Lichfield Commission of the advice given to them by the Legal Advisory Commission of the General Synod that, as the law then stood, 'Baptism is not an essential qualification for the solemnisation of marriages in church.'

ent An Honourable Estate

178.   The law on this matter has not been changed since 1970, though it should be recalled that the Lichfield Report states (para. 280) that

> In 1975 the House of Bishops accepted as a common policy that with regard to marriage by common licence, a licence should not issue where neither party is baptised, and where only one party is baptised, it should be stated in the application form that the other party does not reject the Christian faith and desires marriage in Church. The House felt able to make this rule because a common licence is a privilege granted by the Church and not a right of the parties.

This means of course that the right of unbaptised parishioners to be married in church is related to the calling of banns and not to the common licence procedure, and it may well be that some clergy are not entirely clear about this distinction. From some of the evidence given to us, it seemed that an assumption was being made occasionally that, within the banns procedure also, a clergyman could properly require that one at least of the prospective partners should be baptised. This is not so in English law.

179.   Notwithstanding the legal position concerning the right of un-baptised persons wishing to marry in church, in the evidence we received, the theological argument for Option III was strongly put to us, as it was to the Lichfield Commission. It is said to be inconsistent for the Church to allow those who are not baptised, and are therefore not giving an indication of a desire to be associated with the faith of the Church, to make promises in the context of the demands of Christian worship. The requirement of Baptism for at least one of the parties would serve to give more credibility to marriages conducted in church. Some have suggested that couples should be given the opportunity to make an affirmation of faith before marriage, even if the necessity of Baptism were not pressed.

180.   We recognise the importance of helping couples to understand and respond to the meaning of the marriage service. That is a necessary part of good preparation. We believe, however, that to try to resolve the problem of couples who happen to be parishioners making casual use of a Christian service by requiring Baptism for one of the parties would introduce confusion. Baptism is the primary sacrament of Christian initiation, and of course to be highly commended to all people in its own right, but not we believe to be imposed as a condition precedent to all marriages in church. To impose it would, we believe, be to encourage misunderstandings both of Baptism and of marriage.

70

181.   Equally, we hold that God's gift of marriage to men and women may be received with enjoyment and success whether or not they have been baptised. In terms of divine gift, the institution of marriage which is entered into in the context of a church ceremony is not to be distinguished from a marriage entered into in a civil context. As we have said in Chapter 1 (para. 29), it would be a major and radical shift of theological approach by the Church of England, and a departure from the teaching contained in the Book of Common Prayer, to suggest that marriage is exclusive to Christians or an exclusively Christian institution. The Church should not, we believe, take any action with regard to Baptism before marriage which might be interpreted in this way.

182.   That stressed, we take seriously that, associated with this theological argument, there is a profound pastoral concern of clergy to work where they can for signs of at least minimal Christian perception among those whose marriages they are asked to solemnise. It will often be the case that those coming for preparation who are not regular members of the worshipping community will have had little or no previous contact with the Christian faith as a living tradition. The actual process of preparing for and marrying in church may be highly influential towards faith and discipleship if handled with thoroughness and sensitivity. It is not in fact uncommon, particularly in urban parishes, for adult candidates for Baptism and Confirmation to emerge predominantly from the work of the pastor and his trained laity in marriage preparation. This cannot be forced, nor insisted on, but it is an opportunity for mission not to be underrated.

183.   If a baptismal condition for marriage in church were required by the Church of England the distinction it would attempt to make would be essentially artificial. From the point of view of individuals who are not practising Christians it seems to them to be a matter of chance whether or not they were baptised as infants as a result of parental or family decision. There are many baptised people whose potential as Christians has so far remained, in effect, dormant. They are to be found perhaps more frequently in the rural areas where folk religion led once to their Baptism and now brings them back to the church for marriage. There are many others, an increasing number, who for negative or positive reasons were never brought to Baptism. The good pastor will feel equally concerned for both groups. It would not be helpful to him if he were obliged, or even merely encouraged, to make a distinction between these people on grounds which, in this context and from their

point of view, are 'accidental'. It therefore seems to us that a duty, or even a right, to refuse marriage in church to the unbaptised would be a hindrance, not a help.

OPTION IV

To Introduce Universal Civil Preliminaries

184.   The effect of this option would be to leave all the requirements preliminary to marriage to the civil authority. Anyone wishing to marry in the Church of England would first have to obtain a certificate (with or without a licence) from a superintendent registrar, like those wishing to marry in any other church, and the publication of banns or the issue of a common licence would no longer be legally necessary. This would not affect the conduct of the marriage itself; couples would still have the same entitlement to marriage in the Church of England as they have at present.

185.   This is not the first time that this question has been raised. In 1973 the Law Commission put forward a similar proposal in their Report on the Solemnisation of Marriage. A working party (whose report the Commission adopted) said:[1]

> We have assumed that the purpose of a sound marriage law is to ensure that marriages are solemnised only in respect of those who are free to marry and have freely agreed to do so and that the status of those who marry shall be established with certainty so that doubts do not arise, either in the minds of the parties or in the community, about who is married and who is not. To this end it appears to us to be necessary that there should be proper opportunity for the investigation of capacity (and, in the case of minors, parental consent) before the marriage and that the investigation should be carried out, uniformly for parties to all marriages, by persons trained to perform this function. We suggest that the law should guard against clandestine marriages, that there should be proper opportunity for legal impediments to be declared or discovered, that all marriages should be publicly solemnised and that the marriage should be duly recorded in official registers.

186.   The Law Commission concluded that these aims could be achieved only if the superintendent registrar's certificate became the legal authorisation to marry. This view, however, must be set in the wider context of the Commission's proposals for reform of other aspects

---

[1] Law Commission No. 53, Annex, para. 4

of the law relating to preliminaries, for which they regarded as axiomatic the need to introduce a uniform procedure applicable to all marriages. They asserted that the question of preliminaries fell within the sphere of the civil law and the civil authorities considered that the calling of banns was unlikely to be as effective a way of disclosing impediments as a civil system combining the publication of a notice of intention to marry with investigation of the parties' legal capacity to marry by personnel specially trained for this task.

187.   The Church of England had responded to an earlier working paper which contained some detailed criticisms not embodied in the later report. Two groups set up by the then Archbishop of Canterbury to consider the implications of the proposals in the working paper submitted a joint report which was published as GS Misc. 25. The groups stated that they 'would be opposed to any procedures which could be interpreted as a diminution of the centuries old responsibility of the Church in solemnising marriages and carrying out the necessary civil preliminaries thereto'. Their main reasons for rejecting the suggestion that there should be universal civil preliminaries were:

(a) There is a danger that the proposal would lead to a compulsory civil marriage ceremony which the Law Commission themselves regarded as its 'logical sequel'.

(b) There was insufficient evidence that clergy had failed to fulfil their duties in carrying out the existing law.

(c) Whilst the calling of banns has admittedly broken down as a means of publicising an impending marriage in certain areas, it is no less effective than notice in a register office, whilst in country areas it still has its usefulness and is more effective than a notice.

(d) Clergy are more generally available than superintendent registrars, particularly after normal office hours and at weekends.

(e) The common licence procedure is very flexible and can be used with complete justification when speedy action is called for. It is exercised in a responsible fashion and there is little room for abuse. The care taken before a licence is issued has particular advantages if one party to the intended marriage is a foreigner, when the chancellor may advise on what special precautions should be taken to ensure that the marriage will be recognised as valid by the law of that party's country.

188.   We support this view and believe that these arguments are as valid today as they were then. In particular, in so far as the purpose of

the preliminaries to marriage is to give an opportunity for the investigation of legal capacity and parental consent, the publication of banns and discussions between the parties and a clergyman in preparation for the marriage are in our opinion more likely to bring any impediment or irregularity to light than the giving of notice to a superintendent registrar and its display in a register office. Even wider publicity of an intended marriage would be given by the adoption of the Archbishop's groups' suggestion that banns should be displayed on a notice board after first publication.

189.   We must stress the importance of proper training of clergy in the carrying out of their legal duties in these matters. We recommend that training for these tasks be included in post-ordination and in-service training for clergy. We further recommend that the skills and experience of the registration service be used for this purpose.

190.   We are conscious that the visit of a couple to the church to arrange for banns to be published or to make arrangements for a licence to be issued may be the first opportunity given to the Church for offering pastoral care. It is our view that the Church should not be seeking to reduce the opportunities that it has to welcome and help couples preparing for marriage. The Law Commission pointed out that the Church could insist on the publication of banns (or the granting of a licence) as an additional ecclesiastical formality if it wished. But couples benefit from the present system since they are able to deal with the legal requirements and with the arrangements for their wedding service together. If they wish to be married in the Church of England all these matters can be dealt with in one place. A couple are able, at the time they fix the date of a proposed marriage, to settle dates for the publication of banns and for further sessions in preparation for the marriage. The introduction of universal civil preliminaries would involve couples seeking marriage in the Church of England in making separate arrangements for the preliminaries and for their wedding service. We see no strong argument for such a change, which would do nothing to allay the anxieties of those concerned at the general right to be married in one's parish church. There are, moreover, as we have indicated, a number of practical reasons against it.

OPTION V

To Affirm the Present Position and to Make Full Use of the Opportunities it Offers to the Church

191.   With all those who have advocated changes in the legal position

of the Church of England in these matters we share a concern that the Church should give a clear witness to the Christian understanding of and vision for marriage (see para. 119). We share many of the anxieties about aspects of our present social experience of marriage in England today. We have certainly experienced an increasing shift, in much of the life and thinking of ordinary people, away from the teaching and values of the Church. There is growing diversity in the ways in which people organise their lives and in what their goals and aims are. The sources of moral values and personal and corporate standards are many and various and include other faiths and atheistic or agnostic philosophies. In such a changing setting the Church has to consider how best to respond in a faithful living out of its mission.

192.   It is important that careful and dispassionate consideration be given to all the options lest the Church makes the wrong responses to the present challenge. We are convinced that changes in the position of the Church of England in its present duties, in connection with marriage, would be the wrong response. The problems would remain and the opportunities for the Church to make a constructive contribution to helping our society affirm and uphold a wholesome understanding of marriage would be lessened. Furthermore, we see a temptation in trying to resolve the theological debate in the Church concerning marriage and divorce by adjusting the duties of the Church in society. The resolution of such matters can only take place by honest enquiry and debate within the Church.

193.   It would be false, however, to suggest that the type of question we face today is basically different from that which has troubled the Church in past ages. Indeed, the evidence would suggest that there have been significant periods in our history when the Church has had to struggle to have more than a marginal role in the whole business of marriage in society. It would be wrong to suggest that up until recent times the Church had a dominant and central role in determining the patterns of social life surrounding marriage. The Hardwicke Act of 1753 was, at least in part, designed to bring a disordered situation under greater control. The patterns of courtship, marriage and family life were rooted deep in the class culture of our society and derived as much of their life and rationale from patterns of social need as from any understanding of Christian belief. Adjusting the position of the Church of England concerning its duty to conduct the marriage ceremonies of those, with the exception of divorced people whose former partners are still living, who are entitled in law to be married, would not meet the

main issue. We would still be left to consider how to respond to the changing patterns of the way couples approach marriage and the changing perceptions about what place and meaning marriage has in their experience.

194.   There have been some important shifts in attitudes and practice surrounding marriage, as the statistics set out in Chapter 4 show. Not all of these are welcome and some do represent a serious departure from Christian values. Christians worry about divorce statistics and cohabitation and it is important to form a sober and careful judgment on these issues. It would be easy to take an unduly pessimistic and gloomy view on the basis of these real and distressing trends. Yet it remains the case that in spite of recent major shifts in our culture and the existence of more liberal divorce laws and greater longevity, the great majority of marriages are still ended by death rather than divorce, and those who do experience the trauma of divorce, far from abandoning the institution of marriage, return to it again.

195.   The Law Commission has stated (in Paper 112) 'We believe that it is in the interests of Society that the institution of marriage be respected and that divorce be regarded as regrettable.' As a group we believe that Parliament has a duty to support the institution of marriage. The Church should continue to press policy-makers and governments to ensure that changes in the law and in social policy have the effect of upholding the institution of marriage and encouraging couples and families to succeed in their mutual commitments. These obligations extend beyond marriage to the family. The well-being of children is bound up with the health of the institution of marriage and the family in our society. We have been particularly concerned about the apparent lack of an overall and coherent policy for the family in Britain, which would require careful attention to the impact on family life of all major developments in public policy. In our view, the Church can exert pressure most successfully from its position of strength afforded by its current involvement in the legal processes of marriage. Once the Church allows herself to be marginalised in respect of these processes, it will be easier and more tempting for policy-makers and governments to ignore the Church's contribution to debate. Especially will this be so if it appears to them that the Church is asking for changes that are inconvenient for, or contrary to, their policies in other areas, such as taxation or housing. A society in which marriage is a popular and much used institution offers the Church considerable opportunities to press for support and help to be given to it at all levels.

196.   Similarly, the fact that so many seek the ministry of the Church at the time of their marriage opens the way for the Church to contribute to public understanding, through the education, care and support it offers at such moments. In our work we have been made aware of the ministry of pastoral care offered in many of our churches, often and increasingly by lay people. We need to continue to train and support clergy and lay people in the whole ministry of marriage education, preparation, enrichment and support, not just at the time of marriage, but for all age groups, so that well-grounded attitudes to marriage are fostered from an early age.

197.   It would give quite the wrong impression to society for the Church of England to ask to be relieved of these responsibilities at this time of so much need. It would be impossible to affirm convincingly that marriage is one of God's greatest gifts to all people, whatever their personal faith and social background. The pastoral consequences of such changes would be confusing. The Church must not imply that there are two sorts of marriage, a first-class marriage for those who pass the Church's test, and a second-class marriage for everyone else. To do so would be to create, by our own act, two classes of marriage in our society; it would be a self-fulfilling prophecy.

198.   For centuries, the Church of England has willingly offered Christian ministry to all who are prepared to receive it. Marrying people is one aspect of this ministry. To alter this would suggest that the Church is no longer willing or able to carry forward its mission. It would represent a serious loss of nerve.

APPENDIX 1

The Marriage of the Unbaptised

1.   The most recent treatment of the common law rights to marriage of the unbaptised is contained in paras 200–210 of the Report 1970 *Church and State* as follows:

200   The law of marriage is not certain. It appears probable, that if the other conditions of marriage are fulfilled, any two citizens of the country can claim to be married in their parish church and the incumbent has no right to refuse to marry them. This dates from the period when the only legal marriages, except for Quakers and Jews, were those celebrated in parish churches, and when except for Quakers and Jews almost everyone was baptised by Christian rites. But (in theory) a minister could probably be compelled to celebrate the marriage of two unbaptised persons.

This oddity has been referred to your Commission by the two Convocations at a session of 10 October 1966.

201   The Canon Law Commission of 1947 introduced a draft Canon which forbade the marriage in church of two unbaptised persons, and reserved to the bishop's discretion the cases where one of the two parties was not baptised. The Convocations and the House of Laity approved the draft Canon virtually without opposition. If one opinion of the law of England is correct, the Canon could not be implemented without the approval of Parliament.

202   The point has been declared to be 'largely academic'. Certainly we cannot imagine two persons, both of whom are unable to accept baptism, suing a minister because he felt himself unable to marry them.

203   We doubt whether the proposed Canon is in the best interests of the Church. Its real effect is less to remove from the unbaptised the right to be married in church than to remove from the parish minister the right to marry such persons at his pastoral discretion. Even from the debate which referred this question to us, it is clear that some ministers would regret the removal of their discretion. In that debate a speaker quoted the instance of members of the Salvation Army. Certainly it would make an odd Canon which on the one hand refused all discretion to the minister to consider the case of two persons who wholly accepted the Christian view of marriage but (perhaps by the accident of upbringing) have not been baptised, while on the other hand it compelled him to marry two persons who

78

repudiated the Christian view of marriage but happened (perhaps by the accident of upbringing) to have been baptised as infants.

204 But although the proposed Canon is open to these objections, we consider some change in the law is desirable. It would be repugnant to large sections of Anglican opinion if marriages, where both parties were unbaptised, must by law be solemnised according to the rites of the Church of England, if the parties so desired. For at every turn the marriage service assumes that the parties are, by baptism, members of Christ's body. We believe the best way to deal with the matter would be to place the solemnisation of such marriages at the discretion of the minister guided by such regulations as may be made from time to time by the General Synod. He should not, by law, be compelled to solemnise such a marriage, but he should not, by law, be prevented from doing so, if he considers it warranted by the pastoral situation of the parties concerned. Parliament would be asked to adopt the same policy in regard to marriages in church where both parties are unbaptised, as it had already adopted in regard to marriages in church of those whose previous marriage has been dissolved and whose previous spouse is still living. In the adjustments of the relationship between Church and State, which our Report proposes, we are of the opinion that the question of marriages in church, where both parties are unbaptised, should not be overlooked.

205 Nevertheless, though we hope that the General Synod will not enact the particular Canon which is proposed, we believe that this is essentially a spiritual matter, and the General Synod should have the right to pass such a Canon if on mature reflection it considers it to be the Christian course of action. The State has an interest in the solemnity of marriage, and to that extent has an interest in the work which the Churches perform in celebrating marriages. But the question whether a man and a woman are such that a Church may properly solemnise their marriage is one which their Church should determine. It can hardly be the State's interest to encourage those who do not accept the Christian view of marriage to use forms of words which make them profess publicly a view of marriage which they do not accept.

206 This question of the discipline of baptism touches another such question, which you have not referred explicitly to this Commission, but which is so parallel that it seems to go hand in hand. The minister has a legal obligation to baptise any baby which is brought to him by a parishioner. This dates from the time when the baptism was also (in effect) the civil registration. And on first sight the Church ought to hesitate before encouraging a minister to baptise a baby whose parents have every intention of not bringing him up in the Christian way and whose intention in bringing him to baptism is therefore in doubt. The modern State has no interest in such a question.

207 Such a law was in origin undoubtedly a law of the Church, and only became a law of the State because it was a law of the Church. A rule made

for a time when nearly everyone had the intention of bringing up their children as Christians needs change in an age when not everyone has this intention.

208 The administration of baptism, and its consequences so far as they concern marriage or funerals,* are spiritual matters which should rightly be determined by the authorities of the Church of England.
At present the law forbids the funeral service to be used for those who die unbaptised.

209 Into the enabling Measure which we propose–that is, the Measure which under safeguards permits the General Synod to determine the prayers of the Church of England–it would be possible to insert a clause giving the General Synod similar powers over the administration of baptism and its consequences for marriage and funerals.

210 Nevertheless we recognise that the problems of marriage and baptism cannot be solved in terms of rules and rights, but in the setting of pastoral care.

2.   No legislation since 1970 has affected the question. In February 1986 the following question was asked in General Synod:

QUESTION

'AS (i) the last rubric of The Order of Confirmation (BCP) states, "And there shall none be admitted to the Holy Communion, until such time as he be confirmed, or be ready and desirous to be confirmed"; and

(ii) the last rubric of The Form of the Solemnisation of Matrimony (BCP) states, ". . . the new-married persons should receive the Holy Communion at the time of their Marriage, . . ."; and

(iii) prior to the first Marriage Act of 1753 (now repealed) a valid marriage contract did not need to take place *in facie ecclesiae*; and

(iv) since the Marriage Act 1836 the pre-1753 position is restored via the civil Register Office ceremony;

WHAT authority exists, save purported custom, that obliges any priest to solemnise any marriage according to the rites of the Church of England of persons other than those who ". . . be confirmed, or be ready and desirous to be confirmed"?'

ANSWER

'I would refer Mr Whitmey to Paragraph 200 of the Church and State Report 1970 where it is stated: "it appears probable, that if the other conditions of the marriage are fulfilled, any 2 citizens of the country can claim to be married in their parish church and the incumbent has no right to refuse to marry them." I will refer this question to Sir Timothy Hoare's Marriage Group.'

3.   The Legal Adviser to the General Synod has commented on this question and answer as follows:

(1) 'In a question to the Secretary-General at the February 1986 Group of Sessions, Mr Whitmey suggested that no priest of the Church of England was obliged to marry persons other than those who are confirmed or are ready and desirous of being confirmed. In support of this proposition he referred to the following facts—

 (i) the last rubric of The Order of Confirmation (BCP) states,

"And there shall none be admitted to the Holy Communion, until such time as he be confirmed, or be ready and desirous to be confirmed";

(ii) the last rubric of The Form of the Solemnisation of Matrimony (BCP) states, ". . . the new-married persons should receive the Holy Communion at the time of their Marriage . . .";

(iii) prior to Lord Hardwicke's Act of 1753 a valid marriage contract did not need to take place *in facie ecclesiae*; and

(iv) since the Marriage Act 1836 the pre-1753 position had been restored via the civil Register Office ceremony.'

(2) Answering Mr Whitmey, the Secretary-General referred him to Paragraph 200 of the Church and State Report 1970 which states that 'it appears probable, that if the other conditions of the marriage are fulfilled, any two citizens of the country can claim to be married in their parish church and the incumbent has no right to refuse to marry them.'

(3) If one turns first to the text books, Phillimore (1895) says

'Marriage between Christian and non-Christian has in fact been deemed lawful, notwithstanding the *cultus disparitas*, though always more or less discouraged. When the non-Christian was a Jew, the discouragement has at times amounted to prohibition and punishment. Even then the union was not necessarily invalid.'

Cripps on Church and Clergy states

'The intervention of a clergyman in marriage is now at the option of the contracting parties . . . Marriage therefore is no longer necessarily the subject of ecclesiastical cognisance; . . . but whenever the parties may choose to contract marriage according to the forms of the Church of England, the clergyman is still bound to solemnise it according to prescribed forms and to observe all the laws relating to it' (8th ed., 1937, p.534).

(4) Garth Moore qualifies this to some extent in his book *An Introduction to English Canon Law* as follows—

'It seems probable that every parishioner is entitled to marriage in church after banns, whether the parties are members of the Church of England or not, save possibly where neither party has been baptised' (2nd ed., 1985, p.91).

(5) Tracing the history of the law concerning marriage of the unbaptised is not easy. It is clear from the Canon Law of the Middle Ages that marriage between baptised and unbaptised persons was prohibited. In England the first Prayer Book of Edward VI (1549) provided that 'the new-married persons (the same day of their marriage) must receive the Holy Communion'. The rubric directed the beginning of the Holy Communion after the final blessing of the marriage service, but this direction was expressly omitted in 1662. In the Prayer Book of that year the provision that the new married persons must communicate on their wedding day was modified to read: 'It is convenient that the new-married persons should receive the Holy Communion at the time of their marriage, or at the first opportunity afterwards.' (It should be noted that in his question, Mr Whitmey omitted the words 'it is convenient that'.)

(6) By the nineteenth century marriage by deacons was recognised as lawful (*R. v. Mills* [1844] 717 HL) and this is unlikely to have happened if Holy Communion at the Marriage service had still been the norm.

(7) In the case of *R. v. Moorhouse James* [1850] (19 LJMC 179) it was contended that the words 'it is convenient' in the rubric ought to be construed as words of obligation so that none except those who have been confirmed or are desirous of being confirmed would be capable of being married according to the Prayer Book rite, or, alternatively, that the words should be taken as giving an option to the minister to decline to officiate when neither of these conditions is present. The point was only argued on one side, as the case eventually did not turn upon it.

(8) Turning to Lord Hardwicke's Act of 1753, this provided that all marriages, save those of Jews or Quakers, must take place in the parish church and in no other place, and by inference imposed a duty upon the clergy to marry any of their parishioners. The Act made no reference to baptism or confirmation. For example, if a Jew wanted to marry a baptised person, the marriage had to take place in the parish church. In *Argar v. Holdsworth* (1758) 2 Lee 515, it was held that a minister who without just cause refuses to marry persons entitled to be married in his church commits an ecclesiastical offence for which he is punishable in the ecclesiastical courts.

(9) In the Marriage Act of 1823 all marriages, except those of Jews or Quakers, had to be solemnised in the parish church. In 1836, civil marriages were introduced for those who did not want a Church of England ceremony. The Act of 1836 also authorised a superintendent registrar to issue persons who had complied with the requirements of the Statute, a certificate to stand in place of the publication of banns, 'and every person . . . shall solemnise marriage as after due publication of banns'. It was no part of the superintendent registrar's duty to enquire whether or not the parties had been baptised.

(10) In the case of *Thompson v. Dibdin* (1908–12) [AC 533] Lord Justice Fletcher Moulton said: 'One of the duties of clergymen within this realm is to perform the ceremony of marriage, and parishioners have the right to have the ceremony performed in their parish church. Accordingly the effect of the main enactment (i.e. The Matrimonial Causes Act, 1857) would have been to make it incumbent upon clergymen to perform certain marriages which previously they could not be called upon to perform, and to do such acts as have to be done by clergymen in connection therewith, such as the publication of banns, etc. It was well known that many clergymen held strong dogmatic objections to the marriages thus legalised, and the object of the proviso was to respect their scruples in connection with these newly legalised marriages by relieving them from this obligation . . . By section 57 of the Matrimonial Causes Act 1857, liberty to remarry was given to both parties if the decree of divorce had been made absolute . . . The Act contained the following proviso: 'provided always that no clergyman in holy orders of the United Church of England and Ireland shall be compelled to solemnise the marriage of any person whose former marriage may have been dissolved on the ground of his or her adultery, or shall be liable to any suit, penalty or censure for solemnising or refusing to solemnise the marriage of any such person.' There is no doubt that the protection given by this language was an exceedingly narrow one, because it did not protect the clergyman in refusing to perform acts connected with the marriage, such as publication of banns. But it evidences clearly that the fact of the existence of such scruples on the part of some of the clergy was not sufficient to induce the legislature to make any change in the duties and obligations of clergymen excepting so far as related to the solemnisation of the marriage itself.'

(11) Thus, whatever may have been the case in the Middle Ages or at the Reformation, it would seem doubtful whether it could be argued in 1986 that lack of baptism or confirmation is a legal impediment to marriage according to the rites and ceremonies of the Church of England.

(12) Could it be argued that a 'conscience provision' already exists? There is no evidence for this in the works of the various ecclesiastical lawyers already quoted. For example, Garth Moore (op cit p.39) 'As a corollary to his obligation to attend divine worship, a parishioner has a right of entry to the parish church at the time of public worship . . . He has a right (if it can be so termed) to the burial of his body in the burial ground of the parish, regardless of his religion. He has a right to be married in the parish church, at any rate if one of the parties to the marriage has been baptised. In general, it is apprehended that, whatever his religion, as a parishioner he has a right to the ministrations of the Church, so far as they are appropriate to his condition.'

(13) In 1975 the Lichfield Commission accepted that 'baptism is not an essential qualification for the solemnisation of marriage in church, and that the clergy are not entitled to refuse to marry such persons after due publication of banns'.

(14) The fact that in the Statute Law there is an express power given to the clergy to refuse to marry, for example, divorced persons (Matrimonial Causes Act 1965, s8) inclines one to think that a general conscience provision for clergymen does not exist other than as provided by Statute.

APPENDIX 2

Evidence from the Mothers' Union to the General Synod Law of Marriage Group

INTRODUCTION

The Mothers' Union is a world-wide Anglican Society with a membership of nearly 200,000 in the British Isles, of whom the majority are in England and Wales. The primary purpose of the Mothers' Union is the strengthening and preservation of marriage and Christian family life. It is therefore concerned with all legal and social matters which affect marriage and the quality of family life. Membership is drawn from every section of the community living in rural, urban and suburban areas, representing every shade of opinion, both political and theological, normally to be found in the Church of England. Many members have a professional connection with the Church, either through their husbands or in their own right.

SAMPLE

These comments are based on the findings of surveys carried out in every diocese in England and two dioceses in Wales. In most cases the findings are the result of discussion among a group of members. Occasionally the groups included the incumbent. A small minority of surveys were filled in by individuals on their own. The results therefore are substantially representative of the MU as a whole, which in turn is a fair cross-section of the concerned lay membership of the Church.

GENERAL COMMENT

On all but one question (see below) the majorities were clear and overwhelming; most were more than 80 per cent, two as high as 96.5 per cent. Even in the one question where the minority was larger, it was still only approximately 36 per cent. This question had to do with the suggestion that incumbents should have more choice over whom they marry than at present (see below).

THE QUESTIONS

(Explanations were given in the study papers where necessary. These are a selection of the questions most pertinent to the current enquiry.)

85

Should all parishioners, whatever their religious belief or lack of it, continue to have the right to be married in their parish church?

(N.B. It was made clear that this question applied only to those seeking a first marriage for both.)

The majority were very anxious that this right should continue. From the comments it was obvious that the phrase 'whatever their religious belief' was, on the whole, taken to refer to other Christian denominations rather than other religions; in the same way the phrase 'or lack of it' was, on the whole, taken to refer either to baptised but lapsed Anglicans or to those whose parents were baptised but were not necessarily so themselves. It is therefore probably safe to infer that MU members have not considered, as a major problem, the matter of whether or not adherents to non-Christian religions should have the right to be married in the parish church. Among the comments made in answer to the survey questions the statement that such a right provides an 'opportunity for outreach' or 'mission' occurred over and over again. One group commented that to refuse to marry a couple might have a very adverse effect, not only on the couple themselves, but also on their families and friends. Another said they and their priest were 'very much against trying to "close the door" to anyone and feel that despite the (sometime) abuse of the system it is far more important to be open to everyone and use all opportunities to witness'.

Nearly as prominent was the request for some form of marriage preparation or 'counselling' to help the young couple become more fully aware of the specifically Christian and spiritual content of the service and the ideal of a life-long commitment. This might, so it was hoped, avoid some of the more blatant occasions of the church being merely 'used'. Some groups stressed the difficulties of choosing between one couple and another. One group asked 'By whose authority do we say "no" to a Christian marriage (sic) if requested' and another thought that 'it places the incumbent in an intolerable position if he is expected to pass judgment'. Finally, one group from a very rural deanery commented 'We feel (especially in a village) that the church is and always has been the centre of life.'

Should an incumbent have the right to refuse to marry any couple whom he does not consider it would be appropriate to marry in the parish church?

(We must admit that, as phrased, this question could be ambiguous; several respondents pointed out that clergy, for reasons of conscience, already have the right to refuse to marry a couple, although the parish church must be placed at their disposal.) This was the question where the majority was only approximately 63 per cent and was in favour of retaining the present position, giving the clergy no greater choice than at present over whom they are prepared to marry. Again, it was the judgmental attitude implied that was most disliked and distrusted, carrying, as it must, opportunities for abuse, personal prejudice and variation from parish to parish. The tenor of the replies of the majority was perhaps most succinctly summed up by the group who wrote, 'God is the judge not the incumbent.'

Almost all those who would allow a greater degree of discretion to the clergy commented that a couple whose wedding had been refused should be told the reasons why. It was recognised that it would be difficult to draw up a list of criteria: suggestions ranged from 'the obvious immaturity or incompatibility of the couple' to the fact that one (or both) of them had a criminal record. However, several of those supporting the minority view would want to involve the Bishop in the decision to refuse to marry and would want to give the couple the right of appeal, though no suggestions were forthcoming as to with whom the appeal should be lodged.

Should the laws of England be changed so as to require all couples to be married by the State in a universal civil ceremony?

There was a very strong 'gut reaction' against this suggestion, comments were peppered with exclamation marks and underlining (one group merely said 'No, we are British!'). It obviously aroused very strong feelings among the members as well as reasoned objections, so that over 80 per cent gave a determined 'no' in answer. It was pointed out by more than one group that if a continental style universal civil marriage became the law, some people (not only the couple involved but their friends and relations as well) might never enter a church during the whole of their lives, with the consequent diminution of the Church's opportunities for mission and the fulfilling of 'God's will for the world'. It was also pointed out that to change from the present practice would be 'misunderstood by the occasional church attender and fringe people'. It would, thought another group, 'prolong the actual process of getting married and cause considerable extra expense'.

Among the small minority who would advocate a universal civil ceremony were several who were more concerned with second marriages after divorce than first marriages. They saw this as a way to avoid the distinction between a first marriage where there is a choice of ceremony and a second marriage after divorce where the choices do not include a C. of E. wedding, even though one of the couple is marrying for the first time. If all, regardless of previous status, were obliged to follow the same procedure it would lessen the shame and hurt so often felt ('even after 12 years') when a church service is denied. Other reasons given for advocating such a system were that it would be 'tidier' and would encourage couples to think out their commitment to the Church more coherently. However, this last reason was also given by another group as a reason for retaining the current choice!

Do you think the C. of E. should follow the Roman Catholic practice and only recognise a marriage for a member of the C. of E., if a C. of E. priest is present and taking part in the ceremony, or if the requisite dispensation were to be given for marriage in another Christian church?

An overwhelming majority (96.5 per cent) rejected this suggestion, giving many of the reasons already adduced. Any intimation that the C. of E. might become an exclusive sect, ministering to its own members only, is greatly disliked and repudiated by members.

They were worried about the status of those married before any change in the law–would their marriages cease to be recognised as valid once the law had changed?–about any reaction ecumenically and about any hint of two classes of marriage. The phrase 'second-class marriage' was to be found in many answers.

The Church of England accepts that the vows made at a Register Office marriage are as morally binding as those made at a church marriage. Do you agree with this statement?

An equally large majority (96.5 per cent) agreed with this statement. Not many comments were made, though several groups drew a distinction between vows which were morally binding and those which were also spiritually binding. One group pointed out that the church service is a sacrament as well as the making of a legal contract, but another was firmly of the opinion that 'God is not present in a Registry (sic) Office wedding'. We were also reminded that a Register Office wedding is cheaper than a church service.

Should the Church be prepared to accept Disestablishment in order to obtain a change in the marriage laws?

Again, an overwhelming majority, over 90 per cent, rejected disestablishment for a variety of reasons. The comments from the English dioceses were mainly concerned with our heritage and the position of the monarchy. There was also wide acceptance of the responsibilities implied by being an established Church, 'we honour the concept of the Church's responsibility for all, something which is very close to the fundamental teaching of Christ'. 'The Church of England can be a great power for reason and good in the political life of this country. This is something which cannot be given up lightly.' Many thought a change in the marriage laws far too slight a reason to risk disestablishment. One interesting comment from the diocese of Llandaff was that, despite 60 years of disestablishment, the Church in Wales still has in many places a standing denied to other denominations, especially in the more remote valleys and parishes, with 'the Vicar regarded by all as the leading Christian presence'.

CONCLUSION

This whole subject has obviously touched a sensitive nerve among lay members of the Church. Overwhelmingly they want the status quo retained and no suggestion that any more barriers should be erected by the Church. They are conscious that marriage itself is an option that nowadays not all couples choose. One final quotation, which sums up the general feelings of all:

'Much of the answer to this whole problem lies in adequate and responsible preparation of people intending to marry and a tolerant attitude from the incumbent, remembering that God is always available to everyone, that he rejects no-one, and that our own earthly judgments are not infallible.'

Hazel Treadgold
Central President, Mothers' Union
20th June 1986

Diocese . . . .

THE MOTHERS' UNION

Marriage Group Survey 3

(Delete where not applicable. Please use extra paper, if necessary.)

A.   In England, as the law and practice relating to marriage stands at present, any person has the right to be married in his or her Church of England (C. of E.) parish church whatever their religious belief, or lack of it, providing there is no legal bar ('cause or just impediment') to the marriage.

Providing the marriage will be legal and providing at least one of the couple lives in his parish, an incumbent in the C. of E. has no right to refuse to celebrate the marriage, except where either (or both) of the couple has been divorced and has a living ex-spouse.

A number of clergy are very unhappy with this situation and are seeking a change in the law.

Q1.   *Should all parishioners, whatever their religious belief, or lack of it, continue to have the right to be married in their parish church (C. of E.)?*
YES   NO
Comment, if relevant.

(The following question is *not* concerned with those who have been divorced only those seeking marriage for the first time.)

Q2.   *Should an incumbent have the right to refuse to marry any couple whom he does not consider it would be appropriate to marry in the parish church?*
YES   NO
Comment and explanation, if relevant.

B.   In many European countries the only *legal* marriage is that performed and registered by the State but many couples have a church service of blessing/thanksgiving as well.

Q.   *Should the law in England be changed so as to require* all *couples to be married by the State in a Universal Civil Ceremony?*   *YES   NO*
Comment, if relevant.

C.   The C. of E. has always recognised a Register Office (Registry Office) marriage as a perfectly valid marriage, as morally binding as a church wedding. For its own members, the Roman Catholic Church does not. It will only recognise as a valid marriage for a Roman Catholic, a Christian ceremony in a Roman Catholic church at which a Roman Catholic priest is both present and officiates, unless a specific dispensation has been granted allowing the marriage to take place in another Christian church. It does not recognise as valid for a Roman Catholic a ceremony which takes place in a Register Office.

Q1. *Do you think the C. of E. should follow the Roman Catholic practice and only recognise a marriage for a member of the C. of E., if a C. of E. priest is present and taking part at the ceremony, or if the requisite dispensation were to be given for marriage in another Christian church?* YES NO
Comment, if relevant.

Q2. *The Church of England accepts that the vows made at a Register Office marriage are as morally binding as those made at a church marriage. Do you agree with this statement?* YES NO
Comment, if relevant.

D.   The Church of England is an Established Church. Among other things this means that the clergy assume responsibility for any person living in their parish (parishioner) who does not positively profess another denomination or faith. It is this assumption of responsibility for *all*, by the Church, that gives any parishioner the right (with certain safeguards) to be married in his or her parish church. If the Church seeks to remove these rights from the individual (see Section A) Parliament may well seek to disestablish the Church.

Q. *Should the Church be prepared to accept disestablishment in order to obtain a change in the marriage laws?* YES NO
Comment, if relevant.

Please return this Questionnaire by 25 APRIL 1986 to:

Mrs R. E. Nugee, JP, MA
c/o The Social Concern Department
The Mothers' Union
24 Tufton Street
London
SW1P 3RB.

Please mark the envelope 'Marriage'.

Canons Relating to Marriage

The following are the Canons currently in force relating to marriage:

B 30–36

B 30   Of Holy Matrimony

1.   The Church of England affirms, according to our Lord's teaching, that marriage is in its nature a union permanent and life-long, for better for worse, till death them do part, of one man with one woman, to the exclusion of all others on either side, for the procreation and nurture of children, for the hallowing and right direction of the natural instincts and affections, and for the mutual society, help and comfort which the one ought to have of the other, both in prosperity and adversity.

2.   The teaching of our Lord affirmed by the Church of England is expressed and maintained in the Form of Solemnisation of Matrimony contained in the Book of Common Prayer.

3.   It shall be the duty of the minister, when application is made to him for matrimony to be solemnised in the church of which he is the minister, to explain to the two persons who desire to be married the Church's doctrine of marriage as herein set forth, and the need of God's grace in order that they may discharge aright their obligations as married persons.

B 31   Of Certain Impediments to Marriage

1.   No person who is under sixteen years of age shall marry, and all marriages purported to be made between persons either of whom is under sixteen years of age are void.

2.   No person shall marry within the degrees expressed in the following Table, and all marriages purported to be made within the said degrees are void.

In this Table the term 'brother' includes a brother of the half-blood, and the term 'sister' includes a sister of the half-blood.

The Table shall be in every church publicly set up and fixed at the charge of the parish.

A TABLE OF KINDRED AND AFFINITY

A man may not marry his	A woman may not marry her
mother	father
daughter	son
adopted daughter	adopted son
father's mother	father's father
mother's mother	mother's father
son's daughter	son's son
daughter's daughter	daughter's son
sister	brother
wife's mother	husband's father
wife's daughter	husband's son
father's wife	mother's husband
son's wife	daughter's husband
father's father's wife	father's mother's husband
mother's father's wife	mother's mother's husband
wife's father's mother	husband's father's father
wife's mother's mother	husband's mother's father
wife's daughter's daughter	husband's son's son
wife's son's daughter	son's daughter's son
son's son's wife	son's daughter's husband
daughter's son's wife	daughter's daughter's husband
father's sister	father's brother
mother's sister	mother's brother
brother's daughter	brother's son
sister's daughter	sister's son

B 32 Of Certain Impediments to the Solemnisation of Matrimony

No minister shall solemnise matrimony between two persons either of whom (not being a widow or widower) is under eighteen years of age otherwise than in accordance with the requirements of the law relating to the consent of parents or guardians in the case of the marriage of a person under eighteen years of age.

B 33 Of the Duty of the Minister to Inquire as to Impediments

It shall be the duty of the minister, when application is made to him for matrimony to be solemnised in the church or chapel of which he is the minister, to inquire whether there be any impediment either to the marriage or to the solemnisation thereof.

B 34 Of Requirements Preliminary to the Solemnisation of Matrimony

1. A marriage according to the rites of the Church of England may be solemnised:

(a) after the publication of banns of marriage;

(b) on the authority of a special licence of marriage granted by the Archbishop of Canterbury or any other person by virtue of the Ecclesiastical Licences Act 1533 (in these Canons, and in the statute law, referred to as a 'special licence');

(c) on the authority of a licence (other than a special licence) granted by an ecclesiastical authority having power to grant such a licence (in these Canons, and in the statute law, referred to as a 'common licence'); or

(d) on the authority of a certificate issued by a superintendent registrar under the provisions of the statute law in that behalf.

2.   The Archbishop of Canterbury may grant a special licence for the solemnisation of matrimony without the publication of banns at any convenient time or place not only within the province of Canterbury but throughout all England.

3.   The archbishop of each province, the bishop of every diocese, and all others who of ancient right have been accustomed to issue a common licence may grant such a licence for the solemnisation of matrimony without the publication of banns at a lawful time and in a lawful place within the several areas of their jurisdiction as the case may be; and the Archbishop of Canterbury may grant a common licence for the same throughout all England.

B 35   Of Rules to be Observed as to the Preliminaries and to the Solemnisation of Holy Matrimony

1.   In all matters pertaining to the granting of licences of marriage every ecclesiastical authority shall observe the law relating thereto.

2.   In all matters pertaining to the publication of banns of marriage and to the solemnisation of matrimony every minister shall observe the law relating thereto, including, so far as they are applicable, the rules prescribed by the rubric prefixed to the office of Solemnisation of Matrimony in the Book of Common Prayer.

3.   A marriage may not be solemnised at any unseasonable hours but only between the hours of eight in the forenoon and six in the afternoon.

4.   Every marriage shall be solemnised in the presence of two or more witnesses besides the minister who shall solemnise the same.

5.   When matrimony is to be solemnised in any church, it belongs to the minister of the parish to decide what music shall be played, what hymns or anthems shall be sung, or what furnishings or flowers should be placed in or about the church for the occasion.

B 36   Of a Service After Civil Marriage

1.   If any persons have contracted marriage before the civil registrar under the provisions of the statute law, and shall afterwards desire to add thereto a service of Solemnisation of Matrimony, a minister may, if he sees fit, use such

form of service, as may be approved by the General Synod under Canon B 2, in the church or chapel in which he is authorised to exercise his ministry: Provided first, that the minister be duly satisfied that the civil marriage has been contracted, and secondly that in regard to this use of the said service the minister do observe the Canons and regulations of the General Synod for the time being in force.

2. In connection with such a service there shall be no publication of banns nor any licence or certificate authorising a marriage: and no record of any such service shall be entered by the minister in the register books of marriages provided by the Registrar General.

Evidence Submitted in Writing

The following bodies and individuals have expressed views to us in writing:

The Revd P. Barnett
The Revd R. T. Beckwith
Mr J. Bell
The Revd P. A. Bird
Mr W. L. Bransgrove
Mr P. E. Bridge
The Revd P. R. Brown
Mgr R. Brown
Canon A. W. Carr
The Revd C. T. Catton
Canon P. J. Chandler
The Revd M. S. Cherry
Miss J. Clark
Chancellor T. A. C. Coningsby
The Revd A. P. Davies
The Revd B. Davies
The Revd C. Kevill Davies
The Revd G. Davies
Miss V. E. Davies
Prebendary P. W. Dearnley
Mr M. R. Ewbank
Mr K. Fagan
Mr J. Fairlie
Mr P. George
Gloucestershire Association for
   Family Life
The Revd F. R. Gough
Mr J. C. Hall
The Revd D. M. Hallatt
Mr J. Haskey
Canon M. R. Hodge
Mr D. Hodgson
Mr A. Hoffer
Dr O. Wright Holmes

British Housewives' League
Dss J. Hunt
The Revd P. James
Canon A. T. Johnson
The Revd F. M. Jones
Mr V. T. Jordan
The Revd J. Kerkhofs SJ
Mrs J. Kidd
Mr A. Kilburn
Canon Professor B. Lindars SSF
The Revd B. W. Maguire
Mr R. Massis
Methodist Division of Social
   Responsibility
Professor Basil Mitchell
Miss M. Mitchell
Mr J. Montgomery
Mr J. Moseley
Mr J. B. Mynors
The Bishop of Newcastle
Rear-Admiral H. D. Nixon
The Revd J. R. Packer
The Hon. R. Pomeroy
The Revd E. A. Pratt
Mr D. Price
Miss U. Reed
The Revd V. J. H. Rees
The Revd G. Reid
The Revd R. P. Reiss
Canon D. A. Rhymes
Mr O. Russell
St Albans Diocesan Synod (Motion)
Canon E. Saxon
Mr M. J. Sayer

The Revd B. J. M. Scott
The Revd M. Silverside
The Revd D. D. F. Smith
The Revd M. Smout
Mr N. Spratling
Mrs B. Statham
Mr J. P. Holden Stevenson
Mr L. Stretch
Miss P. Symes
The Revd P. H. Symons
Mr P. A. Taylor
Mr G. P. Theobald

Mr K. M. Trenholme
The Revd J. M. Turner
Mr G. R. Turtle
Mr J. C. Unsworth
Canon S. Van Culin
Dr P. D. Vicary
The Revd A. J. Vincent
Mrs V. H. Viney
The Revd P. E. de D. Warburton
Mrs M. Whalley
Mrs S. Woolrych
Mrs V. R. Wright

In addition we received written statements of their practice from the church authorities in Finland, France (Eglise Réformée), The Netherlands, Scotland, Sweden, USA, Wales and West Germany.

Fr Jan Kerkhofs SJ provided further information of marriage practice in other countries from information available to Pro Mundi Vita.

We acknowledge, with thanks, the translations provided by Mrs Donata Coleman.

We are grateful to:
Canon Dr Gareth Bennett, Fellow of New College, Oxford,
Member of Standing Committee of General Synod
Professor Christopher Brooke, Dixie Professor of Ecclesiastical Studies,
University of Cambridge
and
Professor David McClean, Professor of Law, University of Sheffield,
Chairman of House of Laity of General Synod
for valuable comments on an early draft of this Report.

APPENDIX 5

Oral Evidence

The following were invited to attend to give oral testimony at one of the Working Party's meetings:

His Honour Judge J. Baker }	on behalf of the Roman
Mgr R. Brown }	Catholic Church in England
The Revd P. Barnett	Team Rector of St Paul's, Bristol
Baroness Blackstone of Stoke Newington	Master of Birkbeck College, University of London
The Revd G. Burt	Secretary of the Social Affairs Division of the Methodist Conference
Mr P. J. Butt	
Mr J. Couchman }	Officers and Members of the
Mr E. Tomlinson }	Society of Registration Officers
Mr M. Viccars	
The Revd Peter Chambers	Secretary to the House of Bishops' Marriage Education Panel
The Bishop of Chichester	The Rt Revd E. W. Kemp
Dr Jur Dieter Giesen	Professor für Privatrechtsvergleichung in the Free University of Berlin
Professor Brenda Hoggett	Managing trustee of Nuffield Foundation and member of the Law Commission
Mr John Haskey	Statistician in the Registrar General's Department
The Revd Jan Kerkhofs SJ	Professor in the University of Leuven
The Revd T. Lloyd	Incumbent of Holy Trinity, Wealdstone, Middx
The Rt Revd H. W. Montefiore	Formerly Bishop of Birmingham and Chairman of the General Synod Board for Social Responsibility
Mrs Muriel Nissell	Formerly of the Policy Studies Institute
The Revd J. R. Packer	Incumbent of Wath-upon-Dearne, Sheffield, until 1985, now incumbent of Sheffield Manor

Mr David Price	Registrar of Wandsworth County Court
Canon D. A. Rhymes	Retired incumbent of Woldingham and former member of General Synod
Canon E. Saxon	Retired incumbent of St Ann, Manchester
Mr N. Stephens	Secretary of the Institute of Population Registration
Mrs Hazel Treadgold	Central President of The Mothers' Union
Mr Nicholas Tyndall	Then National Officer of the National Marriage Guidance Council
Mr Malcolm Wicks	Family Policy Studies Centre

Bibliography

PART I WITH REFERENCE TO PARTICULAR CHAPTERS OF THE REPORT

CHAPTER 1

Genesis, Gerhard von Rad, SCM Press
The Man/Woman Relationship in Christian Thought, Sherwin Bailey, Pelican 1979
Sacramentum Mundi, ed. K. Rahner, Burns & Oates
Marriage: Human Reality and Saving Mystery, E. Schillebeeckx, Sheed & Ward 1965
Code of Canon Law (RC), CTS 1984
The Marriage Bond, Helen Oppenheimer, Faith Press 1976

CHAPTER 2

Marriage: Human Reality and Saving Mystery, Vol. 2, E. Schillebeeckx, Sheed & Ward 1965
Church Life in the Thirteenth Century, J. R. H. Moorman, CUP 1945
The Family, Sex and Marriage in England 1500–1800, L. Stone, Weidenfeld & Nicholson 1977, Penguin Books 1979
For Better for Worse; British Marriages 1600–present, R. Gillis, OUP 1985
Nuptial Blessing, K. Stevenson, Alcuin/SPCK 1982
The Knight, the Lady and the Priest: The Making of Modern Marriage in Mediaeval France, Georges Duby, Penguin 1983
Marriage and Love in England 1300–1840, A. MacFarlane, Blackwell 1986
Contrasting Values in Western Europe, Stephen Harding and David Phillips, Macmillan 1986

For details of marriage practice in other countries we are largely indebted to the evidence supplied by Fr Jan Kerkhofs and Dr Dieter Giesen and the written evidence supplied by various Church authorities.

CHAPTER 3

Marriage in Church and State, T. A. Lacey, SPCK 1912 (revised by R. C. Mortimer, SPCK 1947)
Pushing Asunder?, J. W. M. Bullimore, Grove Books 1981
The Report of the Matrimonial Causes Procedure Committee, HMSO 1985

An Honourable Estate

CHAPTER 4

Social Trends 17, 1987 edition, HMSO
OPCS Monitor Marriages, HMSO 1984
OPCS Monitor Divorces, HMSO 1984
Families in Focus, L. Rimmer, Study Commission on the Family
Happy Families?, Study Commission on the Family 1980
The Family Today, Family Policy Studies Centre Fact Sheet 1984
Values and the Changing Family, Study Commission on the Family 1982
Gallup: Belief in Britain and Europe Today, European Value Systems and Study Group
   1982

PART II   OTHER REPORTS AND BOOKS

Putting Asunder: A Divorce Law for Contemporary Society, Report of a Group appointed
   by the Archbishop of Canterbury, SPCK 1966
Marriage, Divorce and the Church, Report of the Archbishop of Canterbury's
   Commission on the Christian Doctrine of Marriage, SPCK 1971
Marriage and the Church's Task, Report of the General Synod Marriage Commission,
   CIO Publishing 1978
No Just Cause, Report of the Archbishop of Canterbury's Group on the Law of Affinity,
   CIO Publishing 1984
Marriage and the Standing Committee's Task, A report setting out a range of procedures
   for cases where it is appropriate for a divorced person to marry in church,
   CIO Publishing 1983
Marriage and the Doctrine of the Church of England, House of Bishops' Marriage
   Education Panel 1985
Brief Encounters, Wesley Carr, SPCK 1985
Family Issues and Public Policy, Study Commission on the Family, Occasional Paper
   No. 7, 1982
Families in the Future, Study Commission on the Family, Final Report 1983
Report of the Inter-Departmental Committee on Conciliation, HMSO 1983
Matrimonial Causes Procedure Committee, Report, HMSO 1983
Time Restrictions on the presentation of petitions for divorce and nullity, Law Commission
   Paper No. 116, HMSO 1982
Christian Marriage, J. Dominian, DLT 1969
Sociology of the Family, ed. M. Anderson, Penguin 1971
To Have and to Hold, D. Atkinson, Collins 1979
Christians and Divorce, Wendy Green, Mowbrays
The Future of the Family, Wendy Green, Mowbrays 1984
Divorce Law Reform in England, B. H. Lee, Peter Owen 1987
Divorce Matters, J. Bourgogne, Roger Ormrod, Martin Richards, Pelican 1986
The War over the Family: capturing the middle ground, B. & P. Berger, Pelican 1983
Articles on 'Marriage' and 'Divorce' by Helen Oppenheimer in *New Dictionary of
   Christian Ethics*, SCM Press 1986

100